EXPLOSION AT
MORGAN

THE WORLD WAR I MIDDLESEX MUNITIONS DISASTER

RANDALL GABRIELAN

Charleston   London

THE
History
PRESS

Published by The History Press
Charleston, SC 29403
www.historypress.net

Copyright © 2012 by Randall Gabrielan
All rights reserved

Cover image courtesy of the Sayreville Historical Society.

First published 2012

Manufactured in the United States

ISBN 978.1.60949.517.6

Library of Congress CIP data applied for.

CONTENTS

FOREWORDS

National issues and historic time periods are often better understood when viewed through the lens of local history. This is true of the disaster at the T.A. Gillespie Shell Loading Plant, discussed by author Randall Gabrielan in his book *Explosion at Morgan*. Providing insight into the war efforts and explaining the contributions of Middlesex County to World War I, this book makes clear that the strategically located county was the hub of munitions activity long before the United States formally entered the war. In fact, Middlesex County toyed with the possibility of siting a large-scale munitions plant as early as 1897, when a German firm purchased land in Spotswood, New Jersey, for this purpose. The project never came to fruition. However, the sale of explosives became a lucrative industry that American businesses were willing to exploit—even at a time when the United States' policy was non-engagement and neutrality.

Mr. Gabrielan tells us that New Jersey was, regrettably, no stranger to fire and explosions at munitions facilities and notes the John Roebling wire-manufacturing plant tragedy in Trenton, the Black Tom Island incident in 1916, the Jersey City Central Railroad incident in 1911 and the 1903 fire at Fort Lafayette in Brooklyn. In 1917, the Gillespie Plant at Morgan (part of Sayreville, Middlesex County) suffered an extraordinary explosion that destroyed the manufacturing operations of this munitions facility and devastated the families of those who perished or were injured. This is a little-known chronicle. The incident is rarely discussed, perhaps because a mere five weeks after the tragedy World War I ended and the nation turned its attention to the process of healing.

Mr. Gabrielan has written an important treatise that explores this misfortune and the period when five thousand Middlesex County workers were employed in various aspects of munitions production, according to a report in the *Times*. The author presents the political, social, industrial and historical context of the explosion, thus framing it in a larger, more critical context. By so doing, Mr. Gabrielan has tackled an inaccessible story, one that raises many questions. He approaches the topic with professionalism and diligence. It is often difficult to write about a disaster and keep an open mind. Early in the discovery stage, one tends to form opinions or assign fault. But Mr. Gabrielan has not fallen into that pitfall and instead presents a story in all its facets, allowing his readers to form their own conclusions. Perhaps this is because Mr. Gabrielan brings a unique and valuable perspective to the study of the Gillespie explosion, informed by his years in the casualty insurance industry. He knows how to look at a catastrophe such as the Morgan explosion/fire and diagnose the elements.

We learn from *Explosion at Morgan* a great deal more than just the history and facts of this single disaster. Four of the five massive plants built to furnish shells for the war effort were located in New Jersey, due in part to the availability of large tracts of open land that had natural buffers between possible facilities and settlement areas and the immediate access to transportation for shipping of raw materials, finished products and even much-needed workers. New Jersey attracted immigrant workers from Russia, Italy and Poland, among other nations of origin, who worked in the munitions factories. Here a lack of fluency in the English language was not an impediment to the performance of repetitive tasks such as those done by factory employees.

We learn that, of the large assembly of workers and inspectors, one-third were women, who it is said, remained longer on the job, performed complex tasks with ease and were better inspectors. They also excelled in record keeping. "Feminists strove to make the point," says Mr. Gabrielan, "that women could do whatever a man could do." Women were praised for their courage, tenacity and fearless approach to dangerous jobs.

The iconic figure of Rosie the Riveter, created more than sixty-five years ago to represent women in the workforce during World War II, endures to this day and is familiar to generations too young to have lived through the war. But Mr. Gabrielan tells us of "Shelley the Shell Loader" from World War I. Her very existence tells us about the female workforce in America from 1914 through 1918. They were offered a wide range of opportunities generated by necessities of war and the need to assign male workers to heavier-burdened tasks or into military service. Sadly, Shelley has passed into obscurity

In terms of safety, it was interesting to learn, workers were told that there was little difference between working in a munitions plant and serving as a soldier on the battlefield—both worker and soldier faced danger everyday at every task. The risk to the Gillespie Plant employees was high, exacerbated by the cramped wooden quarters, the volatile nature of the chemical substances and the additional hazard of an occupational disease called TNT poisoning.

The inherent danger in black powder facilities was made more acute by the saboteurs who infiltrated the workforces and were, as the author states, "bent on destruction." Mr. Gabrielan illustrates this with the story of Kingsland (now the town of Lyndhurst), where the Canadian Car and Foundry Company was located. It was a major supplier of loaded shells to England and Russia prior to the United States' entry into the war. Infiltrators set fire to the plant in order to prevent supplies from reaching the partner nations (which soon would be called the Allies of World War I). Mr. Gabrielan tells us there were no fatalities, in part due to the bravery of Theresa Louise McNamara, who stayed at her post despite spreading flames engulfing the site. One by one, she alerted each of the staff in the company buildings to the peril at hand, giving them precious additional minutes in which to evacuate the premises.

The T.A. Gillespie Shell Loading Plant at Morgan was located on 2,900 acres of land. The owner later reported that 30,000,000 pounds of explosives were stored on the site, plus 1,013,453 loaded shells in magazines, rail cars and operational areas. Most buildings were one-story construction, on a concrete base, although administration, training and loading structures were two or more stories. On Friday, October 4, at approx 7:40 p.m., the horror began with the first large-scale explosion and fire. At 2:00 a.m. the following morning, the fires still burned and the last of the large-scale explosions took place. All through the night, shells whizzed past fleeing workers and molten metal flew through the air, impaling itself into boxcars of T.N.T. Three of these railcars exploded, leaving a crater 6 feet deep,140 feet wide and 150 feet long.

Mr. Gabrielan's extensive research allows him to use firsthand accounts of workers and emergency responders to vividly portray what occurred. We are told of the human cries that punctured the night air, the fire apparatus mobilized from neighboring towns that were hindered from entry to the property, the water-filled moats that encircled each plant as a method to prevent outsiders from gaining access—but which also restricted rescue workers. Of the 700 buildings on the site, 325 were totally destroyed.

Mr. Gabrielan does not end the story with the telling of this fateful night but speaks of the aftermath: the Spanish flu pandemic that was also gripping Middlesex County at the time of the explosion, causing a shortage of hospital beds and healthcare workers, and the attempts to mount a massive relief campaign at a time when federal and state disaster-relief programs had not yet come into being.

Randall Gabrielan's *Explosion at Morgan* adds to the body of knowledge about this tragic event and places it in a broader context. The author has humanized the disaster by including the statements of the plant workers. He identifies them by name and tells us of their backgrounds. He adds bits of information that transform them from factory workers and inspectors to people who are our neighbors and friends.

Anna M. Aschkenes
Executive Director
Middlesex County Cultural and Heritage Commission

Anna M. Aschkenes is the author of five publications on local and New History and is responsible for the award-winning Cornelius Low House/Middlesex County Museum and the historic East Jersey Olde Towne Village. Ms. Aschkenes created the first and only full-time folk life program in the state and is one of the founders of the Cultural Access Network. Her most recent undertaking is the creation of the American Indian Center, located at the lodge in Thompson Park (Jamesburg/Monroe).

New Jersey was a major contributor in the "Arsenal of Democracy" during the Great War, later to become known as World War I. During this time, seven munitions plants were located in Sayreville, with the largest of them all, the T.A. Gillespie Loading Company, situated in the historic Morgan section. Five weeks before the end of the war, Gillespie's Morgan plant was virtually destroyed by a weekend-long series of cataclysmic explosions and fires. In the nearly one hundred years since, this tragic event has been all but forgotten; in fact, most of the current residents living on the grounds of this one-time munitions plant are blissfully unaware of its lethal legacy. In his *Explosion at Morgan*, Randall Gabrielan, noted Monmouth County historian, pieces together the largest and most comprehensive collection of written accounts of the Morgan and other New Jersey munitions-related catastrophes as only he could have done.

Verne James
Owner of "All About Morgan, NJ," www.morgan-nj.org

ACKNOWLEDGEMENTS

I extend my heartfelt thanks to the many who assisted with a project that not many years ago I thought not able to be accomplished. The first thank you is to the Sayreville Historical Society and Jason Slesinski, who provided my first major access into the historical record as he was working on his own fine book, which is cited in the bibliography. The society also provided a number of images. Great thanks go to Verne James, Morgan native, who researches, writes and owns the All About Morgan, N.J. website. While harboring his own plans to write about Morgan, Verne offered great assistance and the utmost in collegial cooperation. Patrick J. Owens, PhD, historian at Picatinny Arsenal, was always ready to respond to a variety of inquiries about munitions. Alycia Rihacek, president of the Madison Township Historical Society (Old Bridge), served as a fine resource for local questions, as did Joyce Elyea for Sayreville and South Amboy. Joan Berkey shared her National Register nomination for the Bethlehem Steel Loading Company (Belco) Archeological District in Atlantic County, which is a fine resource. Frank Yusko's recording of survivors' stories was the first substantive work on the Gillespie explosion.

For sharing of photographs, I thank John Ruszala, as well as his father, Anthony, for his dedicated preservation of striking post-disaster images and the Special Collections and University Archives, Rutgers. I offer a special thank you to Marie Labbancz for sharing her grandfather's picture and helping put a face on the Gillespie disaster. Thank you to the librarians who assisted, especially Pamela Curchin of Middletown and Cynthia Harris of Jersey City. Thanks to the many who shared information, including Al Baumann, Ken Durrua, Tom Gallo, Meredith Luhrs, Mark Nonestied, Kate Philbrick, Art Rittenhouse and Joel Rosenbaum and those not mentioned by name. Thank you to those who shared personal memories of the area and their experiences, including Ken Elyea, Joseph Grabas, Frank Ludlow, Peter McIntyre, Everett Mercer and Michael Zazzarino.

Anna Aschkenes has built the largest county cultural and heritage commission in the state. She has long served as Middlesex's executive director, an organization with outstanding accomplishments overseeing historic sites and mounting exhibitions, public programs and publications. I thank her for writing the book's foreword.

INTRODUCTION

On October 4, 1918, at approximately 7:40 p.m., an explosion ripped through production building no. 6-1-1 at the T.A. Gillespie Shell Loading plant in the Morgan section of Sayreville. The blast killed nearly everyone inside, while the fire that followed spread rapidly and caused secondary explosions, which destroyed the manufacturing operation of the massive munitions plant and rained widespread devastation. While the fire raged out of control, fears were raised that if flames reached the main storage magazines, a blast could follow with a force sufficiently powerful to level a wide surrounding area and result in significant damage as far away as New York

This explosion, the last of a series in New Jersey during World War I, was the state's most catastrophic in terms of loss of life. The number of deaths was probably a minimum of one hundred, but the true toll will never be known. The disaster has been inexplicably forgotten by history or at best reduced to a minor footnote. Timing probably prompted the country to overlook Gillespie. When the misnamed "War to End All Wars" ended only five weeks later, a nation rushing to recovery simply sowed the seeds of forgetfulness.

Reconstruction of the destroyed manufacturing facility began immediately but was halted by the end of hostilities. Peace and demobilization brought new weapons-handling challenges as massive amounts of unused ammunition were returned from Europe in quantities that would strain stateside storage capabilities. While Gillespie's shell-loading capabilities were destroyed, the

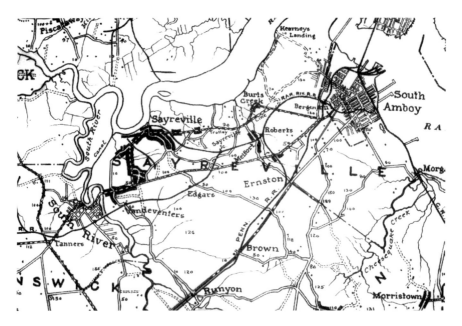

The Morgan locality at the extreme southeastern part of Sayreville led to the perception that the area was hardly a consciously thought of part of that municipality. This perception led to South Amboy claiming, as part of its designs to regain the territory, that it was naturally a part of that city.

plant's largely intact warehouse facilities were transformed into a storage terminal. The function changed, but death from sudden explosion remained a constant risk. There was no early farewell to arms at Morgan as this plant, along with other nearby munitions facilities, continued to demonstrate Middlesex County's sacrifice and role as an arsenal for the Great War, a role that did not end with peace.

Military oversight of the storage terminal lasted about five years. However, memories of the Morgan disaster were regularly revived by ensuing explosions and the discovery of old ordnance. The uncovering of buried ordnance continued for decades. The major remediation effort undertaken in 1994 was intended to end this issue, but knowledgeable residents know that material from that awful event remains in the ground.

It is unimaginable how such a catastrophe remains so little known. The obscurity, forgetfulness and inaccessibility of substantive information has long both puzzled and fascinated me. In time, the confluence of forgetfulness and newly available material became the motivation to research and write this book. The story is told in the context of the Sayreville political landscape, the makeup of the area, other regional and wartime munitions events and the disaster's aftermath.

The writing of the narrative drew from numerous sources, including the news accounts necessary for the unfolding drama as experienced at the time and government reports essential for carefully wrought analysis. At least two major tendencies are behind differing news accounts. First, the total area under bombardment and fire was so vast that most who spoke saw only a small part of it. Second, my long experience in the casualty insurance business taught me that after an accident, claim or suit, some persons directly involved are inclined to lie or distort the facts in order to enhance their own interests.

1

MORGAN IN SAYREVILLE BOROUGH, MIDDLESEX COUNTY

Morgan, the locale of the massive T.A. Gillespie Shell Loading plant, is the easternmost section of the Borough of Sayreville, a 16.3-square-mile municipality. The borough's borders are largely waterways, which include the south bank of the Raritan River on its north, Raritan Bay on the east, Cheesequake Creek on the southeast and the South River on the west. Only two roads that border Old Bridge, Bordentown Avenue and Ernston Road, prevent Sayreville, along with its neighbor to the north, South Amboy, from being an island. The Morgan area's rich and ancient history predates the founding of the Sayreville home municipality. Morgan's history originates with the purchase of an extensive tract by its patronymic Morgan family, their participation in the Revolution and their importance to the early New Jersey pottery industry. Five Morgans served in that war, including Captain James Sr., who commanded a company at a number of sites; three are buried in the local Morgan family cemetery,[1] which was once proposed for designation as a national shrine by Roy Everson, a descendant of General Morgan's wife, according to the *Matawan Journal* of October 2, 1947. Their clay holdings were extensive, while the kiln was located along today's Highway 34 in Old Bridge. Subject of an archaeological study in the recent past, the place has been sealed and is no longer accessible. Morgan as a locality name was first used in 1875 as the designation of the small New York and Long Branch Railroad station located there in a sparsely settled area but one crucially situated at the site of the line's drawbridge over Cheesequake Creek. A contemporary press account noted that an

The establishment of a station there when the New York and Long Branch Railroad opened in 1875 is the first known use of Morgan as a place name. The station is pictured on a circa 1910 postcard.

earlier choice of station name was Cheesequake. However, I believe that the eventual name was selected immediately prior to the start of service for its more euphonious quality.[2]

The significance of clay to Morgan family enterprises was underscored by the family's first transaction with the railroad. In 1872, James R., Theodore B. and their wives, along with Charles and Laurence Morgan, gave a sixty-six-foot right of way to the New York and Long Branch. The line was permitted to slope the sides of this strip so clay and soil would not fall in the way of the rails. However, if usable clay and sand was to be dug in the process, it would belong to the Morgans. The transaction was recorded in *Middlesex Deeds*, Book 134, on July 18 that year.

Middlesex County was established in 1683, when the province of East Jersey was formally organized into its four original counties. The county embraces the northerly start of the Inner Coastal Plain, which contains rich clay deposits, an area that begins around Woodbridge and extends in a southwesterly direction into the Trenton area in Mercer County. The east of Middlesex is bisected by the mouth of the Raritan River, a place where one of the county's earliest municipalities, Perth Amboy, became an important port of entry. The city's stature in the early colony is reinforced by its choice as the residential seat of New Jersey's royal governors. The gubernatorial home, the Proprietary House at 149 Kearny Avenue, is now owned by the State of New Jersey, operated by the Proprietary House Association and open to the public. Listed on the National Register of Historic Places, the Proprietary House is one of central New Jersey's most important historic sites.

The historic boundaries of South Amboy Township, following separation from Perth Amboy by 1782, began on the south bank of the Raritan opposite Perth Amboy and then extended west and south over a vast area that, over the next century, would be split into numerous other municipalities. The political-municipal machinations of South Amboy directly impacted Morgan into the 1920s. After South Amboy attained significance as a railroad center in the third quarter of the nineteenth century, this role made the township willing, even eager, to shed much of its vast undeveloped outlying territory. Long before Mies van der Rohe's design motto "Less is more" entered common parlance, the South Amboy town fathers reasoned that the reduction of their borders to the region that contained and was near the rail facilities would permit them to retain and spend hefty rail-generated tax revenue in their smaller developed area rather than spread the wealth throughout the sparsely settled areas for infrastructure expense. After South Amboy was successful in shedding Madison Township in 1869, they found

Sayre and Fisher accumulated vast landholdings that contained rich clay deposits. *Courtesy of Sayreville Historical Society.*

Sayre & Fisher was the largest manufacturer of bricks in the world.

an accommodating community leader, James R. Sayre, a partner of Peter Fisher, the co-founders of the Sayre & Fisher Company. Formed in 1850, the firm was accumulating vast landholdings that were rich with clay deposits, which the firm mined as the raw material for its brick-manufacturing business, one destined to become the largest in the world. The firm built a community to accommodate its growing workforce, one that was referenced possessively on an 1876 map of Sayre's Village, as "Sayreville belonging to J.R. Sayre, Jr. and P. Fisher in the Township of South Amboy." They would be eager to seize South Amboy's proffered opportunity to control a separate municipality. Sayreville, carved from South Amboy, was organized as a township on April 6, 1876.

Sayre & Fisher was one of several brick manufacturers in town, but it became the largest in the world. While space permits only a brief entry, it grew while incurring its share of labor strife. The return to peace must have been stressful on the operation in view of a large 1924 strike that was prompted over a proposed or forced cut in wages. The firm, sold by the founders' estates in 1927, continued to manufacture bricks until 1970. Sayre & Fisher ceased operations for a number of reasons that include the decline of brick as a building material and the increased value of its land for other purposes, including housing.

2

THE EARLY EXPLOSIVES INDUSTRY AND GILLESPIE FIRM

The American gunpowder industry was established by DuPont on the Brandywine Creek in the early nineteenth century. The experience there made known and reinforced the two essentials of volatiles: handle them with extreme care and separate the facilities in order to reduce loss when accidents, which appeared inevitable, occurred. DuPont built a massive business empire, but powder and explosives had been cottage industries for much of the nineteenth century. Prior to the regulation of land use, the manufacture of powder and explosives could be undertaken nearly anywhere. Most manufacturers sought out-of-the-way locales, but they still needed to be close to transportation. Several found New Jersey ideal and established factories scattered throughout the central part of the state.

In Middlesex County, the earliest powder manufacturing appears to have been the Embry and Keyser operation, which was begun in 1805 on the South River about midway between Old Bridge and Spotswood. The plant was destroyed by an explosion in 1833 on a site that later attained notoriety as the Bloomfield Mills.[1]

While some munitions personnel may say it is the nature of explosives to explode, others point out that explosives do not detonate on their own, but their handling causes explosions. Nevertheless, accidental detonations are not only to be expected, but also their recording as a result of their toll likely secured some small powder firms a spot in documented history. Eruptions in Howell in Monmouth County included among the victims Hudson Maxim, one of the brothers of Maxim gun fame, who lost a hand at his Pneumatic

Torpedo and Construction Company. As he held a piece of fulminate (an explosive salt), he placed a second piece on a stove, which sparked and caused an explosion that tore off his hand at the wrist.[2] Sudden death could claim even those engaged in the most prosaic chore. At the Columbia Mill, also in Howell, Clark Chamberlain and John Reynolds were in the process of carrying to a nearby farm field a box of what the *Register* of July 4, 1900, referred to as "nitro-soda." The substance was, perhaps, "sodatol," an agricultural explosive that combined nitrate of soda with TNT to make a formula with about 40 percent of the power of commercial dynamite. The boxed materials, no longer suitable for explosives, still had utility as fertilizer. They were blown to tiny bits when it exploded. The *Register* noted, "The powder mills at Farmingdale (Howell) have been the scene of several fatal accidents within the past few years. Those who work there say that the employees after a time become careless and that if the proper amount of caution were exercised at all times the danger would be considerably reduced." The level of care given by employees would be scrutinized at Morgan after the explosion.

Middlesex was chosen as the site for a major never-built munitions facility in the late nineteenth century. The *Times* reported on September 20, 1897, that the Westphalian-Rhenish Explosives Company of Germany purchased six hundred acres near Spotswood for construction of a powder plant. Its plans failed to reach fruition following objection from the American Powder Trust. This issue over foreign presence resulted in an agreement that would maintain the territorial integrity of the empires of Krupp (Germany) and the United States' DuPont. Other clashes over the world division of the powder and munitions business were revealed in trial testimony in the notable 1908 anti-trust case that resulted in the breakup of DuPont. A second prospective New Jersey explosives operation by an overseas manufacturer was cancelled. A disagreement over the division of the world market was settled before a plant could be completed. The plant was planned by the Nobel Explosives Company of England, an extant firm founded by Alfred, the inventor of dynamite, as a retaliatory gesture for the sale of explosives by the Aetna Powder Company in 1892–93 to a firm in South Africa that was a major customer of Nobel. Peace prevailed when the two reached a better understanding of the division of the world market. This contentious affair was recounted in 1908 during trial testimony in the aforementioned case that broke up DuPont. In Sayreville, four were killed on November 21, 1905, in a laboratory explosion at the International Smokeless Powder Company at Parlin. That firm would build a major presence in the Parlin section of Sayreville.

Thomas A. Gillespie's accomplished contracting firm, which specialized in infrastructure projects, had the expertise to build quickly and operate a wartime shell-loading plant. He is pictured testifying in a post-explosion inquiry.

Thomas Andrew Gillespie was born July 1, 1852, in Pittsburgh to Scottish parents who emigrated from the north of Ireland to that city in 1847. He played a significant role in the development of early twentieth-century infrastructure construction and attained stature that was not

To Our Own Workmen

In the name of the great cause for which every true American is fighting, in one way or another, we thank you for the splendid response you are making to the Third Liberty Loan.

Here are the amounts which the workingmen of our various companies have subscribed up to Friday noon. These amounts will be still greater by tonight.

Think of it! 9,349 men out of 10,254 loan $649,750! If all workmen in the country lend their support as loyally, that will make over a billion dollars from workmen alone!

Aren't you proud? We are. We are proud of the way you are working. We are prouder still of the way you are loaning your money to our country.

Company:	Number of Men Employed:	Number of Men Subscribed:	Percentage Subscribed:	Amount Subscribed:
T. A. Gillespie Loading Co	5,000	4,503	90%	$302,950
International Loading Corp'n	395	322	82%	25,250
The Runyon Corporation	455	370	81%	27,150
Civilian Inspectors, Parlin & Runyon				3,300
T. A. Gillespie Co. (N. Y. Office)	28	28	100%	19,550
Gillespie Manuf'g Corp'n	94	94	100%	8,200
Int'l Steel & Ordnance Co.	967	967	100%	63,000
East Jersey Pipe Corp'n	75	75	100%	4,550
American Shell Company	1,500	1,400	93%	95,450
Gillespie-Hart Company	771	771	100%	48,500
T. A. Gillespie Co. (Pittsburgh and Louisville)	711	574	80%	39,600
Oliver Loading Co.	258	245	95%	12,250
	10,254	9,349	91%	$649,750

Your money is still yours, invested in the biggest and best corporation in the world—the United States of America.

Total subscription of T. A. Gillespie Company and its allied companies to the Third Liberty Loan, including the above employees, $1,500,000.

T. A. GILLESPIE COMPANY
ENGINEERS AND CONTRACTORS
50 Church Street   New York

A May 4, 1918 advertisement gives insight into the extensive Gillespie operation. The munitions firms in the Sayreville–Old Bridge area had related functions, such as the manufacture of different component parts, but details of their operations and even locations are scant.

diminished by his most often cited historical reference: the linkage of his name to the catastrophic explosion at Morgan during World War I. Gillespie's business career, which began in the employ of the Pittsburgh Gas Company, included time with other firms prior to his forming a business in 1879 for the manufacture of iron bolts and similar staple articles. In 1884, "he joined George Westinghouse, Jr. in the development of the natural gas industry in the Pittsburgh district and through that association rose to the position of one of the leading industrialists of the iron city." Five years later, he and his brother organized the contracting firm initially known as T.A. & R.G. Gillespie Company. The firm was later incorporated as the T.A. Gillespie Company and relocated to New York City. Thomas was its president until 1916 and chairman of the board until his death.

The Gillespie firm's output included "locks and dams for the U.S. government on the Ohio River, the St. Lawrence Power Company's works at Massena, N.Y., the plant of the East Jersey Water Co., the Catskill aqueduct, including the deep pressure tunnel under the Hudson River at Storm King, N.Y., the Pittsburgh Water Filtration Works and sections of the Boston and New York City subways."[3]

Gillespie married the former Julia B. Wall in 1875. Their union produced four children: Thomas H., Henry L., Jean and James P. He joined a number of important clubs, was a yachtsman who was elected commodore of the Thousand Islands Yacht Club and served on public bodies in Pittsburgh and West Orange, New Jersey. Gillespie had numerous business interests in addition to the organization or service with his many subsidiary or affiliated companies. He held a trusteeship with the Equitable Life Assurance Society and was vice-president of a Pittsburgh traction company.

The firm's self-congratulatory May 4, 1918 *New York Times* advertisement lauded his workers' purchase of war bonds but also provides a glimpse into Gillespie's widespread operations. East Jersey Pipe was long located in Paterson, while subsidiaries Runyon and Oliver operated in the Sayreville area. The five thousand workers then at Morgan composed the construction crew.

Gillespie's residence, Silver Spring, named by former owner and poet Lowell Mason, was located on the slope of First Orange Mountain in West Orange. He died there on January 27, 1926.

3

A WORLD AT WAR

The assassination of Archduke Franz Ferdinand of Austro-Hungary on June 14, 1914, in Sarajevo by Serbian Gavriou Princip set off a conflict that would engulf a continent. The event has been called the short answer to "How did World War I start?" but in reality, Europe was enmeshed in a series of entangling alliances and mutual defense treaties that merely awaited a spark to flash an eruption. As smaller entities mobilized, European powers that had vowed their defense were compelled to enter the conflict. A decade of unresolved clashes, including the two Balkan wars, left many nations with scores to settle. However, as the potential for a war of unprecedented proportions emerged, and although a number of the combatants realized that the smaller issues did not justify the prospective cataclysm, they saw no way out of their treaties. Some nations went to war reluctantly. On the other hand, Germany not only foresaw war but also had an extensive, well-organized mobilization plan in place, ready to move at the first firing of the guns of August.

The United States resolved to remain neutral as it embraced a policy that followed the nation's long-standing disdain for involvement in overseas conflicts. However, a second influence was a division in an American population that was not solidly behind the British and their Entente allies, which America would eventually join. In addition, the country had a large German population that was not eager for a clash with the fatherland. While most were of unquestioned loyalty to their present homeland, Germany attempted to ferment discord among them. Germany also tried to obtain the return of its nationals whom it claimed were members of the military reserves. Furthermore, significant parts of America's Irish population were hostile to Britain, an animosity that grew more virulent after Britain crushed the Irish rebellion of 1916. The strict laws of neutrality barred partial treatment of either side.

American business would have willingly sold war material and food to either side, but for practical purposes, British control of the seas made this country's commerce in the material of war one-sided. Indeed, when the war broke out in 1914, German vessels sought safety in ports of neutrals rather than risk destruction on the open seas. The British navy not only undertook a campaign to sweep the seas of German ships but also blockaded German ports. Among the ships that fled to the United States, eighty were berthed along the Hudson; their crews were interned for the duration of the war. The sale of explosives to the Entente was big business with an enormous potential for profit for an ostensibly neutral America, as suggested in the total value of explosives exported from the United States. In the three years from 1914 to 1917, their value went from $10,037,587 to $188,969,893 to $717,144,649.[1]

Germany fought back at sea using the submarine, a new type of war vessel. Using stealth and seizing the advantage prior to the development of defensive measures, Germany's U-boats took a horrendous toll on British

The sinking of the RMS *Lusitania* in 1915, with extensive loss of civilian life, was a major event in shaping American public opinion in favor of the Entente, but the ship was, in practical terms, a floating arsenal.

During the dicey days of American neutrality, the German U-53 visited Newport, Rhode Island, for a courtesy call in 1916. When its captain heard the word "quarantine," he then thought that his appearance was not a good idea and promptly left. This U-boat took a heavy toll on Allied shipping.

shipping. American cargo, lives and, at times, even ships were lost in the submarine campaign. While at the outset, Germany sought to use restraint in targeting only enemy vessels, its worsening domestic situation caused by the blockage resulted in it declaring unrestricted warfare in February 1915 for vessels within a defined area around Great Britain. The world was shocked on May 7, 1915, when a German submarine sank the RMS *Lusitania* by a torpedo, killing 1,198 persons. The many American lives lost did not become a turning point to convince the United States to enter the war, but the incident influenced public opinion against Germany. A wary Germany attempted to respect our alleged neutrality but found it difficult to control the risks of submarine warfare. Indeed, in October 1916, Hans Rose, the commander of the German submarine U-53, reasoned he might make a courtesy call at neutral Newport, Rhode Island. On the seventh, he was received by local naval officials aboard an American warship, but the government was quick to evaluate the situation. After the word "quarantine" was voiced, Rose quickly left. The scenario is bizarre when one considers the heavy toll the U-53 inflicted over the remainder of the war.[2]

Germany's reaction to both the blockade and America's one-sided neutrality was a campaign to damage our capability for making the arms to make war. It sent Franz von Rintelen, a naval intelligence officer, to New York

The World War I Middlesex Munitions Disaster

Germans organized the Bridgeport Projectile Company and built this factory to sabotage America's munitions industry by diverting materials from legitimate use and firms—a clever ruse while it lasted. After the discovery of the true nature of their operations, the plant was taken over by the United States as enemy property.

in 1915 to serve as what might have been characterized as a master of dirty tricks in President Nixon's time. In the early twenty-first century, he would be called a terrorist. One of von Rintelen's earliest actions was a masterful act of deception rather than sabotage. Early in 1915, he established the Bridgeport Projectile Company, which acted and gave the appearance as if it were a legitimate, functioning munitions plant. In reality, its purpose and only operation was the disruption of America's arms industry. Bridgeport Projectile accepted orders for munitions that it had no intention of fulfilling. The firm purchased powder, which it destroyed, thereby denying the material to its enemies. It ordered munitions manufacturing machinery with no expectation of taking delivery. Bridgeport exercised contractual agreements that indemnified the manufacturer but precluded it from selling this machinery to others for a specified period, notably to firms that would produce for America or Germany's enemies. The manner in which this Bridgeport deception tied up the capability of the Camden Iron Works is described in the *Times* of November 17 and 23, 1915. While initially successful, the subterfuge would not last long. After the firm's true nature was uncovered, the plant was seized under the enemy property act, and its operation was reorganized as the Liberty Ordnance Company. America took over and enjoyed the rare opportunity of producing arms in a fine plant built by its enemy.

Von Rintelen enjoyed a second early success through a sabotage undertaking that utilized stealth at sea. His plan embraced an insidious device invented by a German chemist, a former military officer who served his fatherland in the United States as a paid spy. Dr. Walter Scheele developed an incendiary

Idle German sailors on the interned North German Lloyd line ship *Friedrich der Grosse* made easily concealed cigar bombs in the vessel's machine shop. Their use as a means of sabotage required dockworkers to conceal them inside the holds of cargo vessels.

device that he built from a lead tube about the size of a long cigar, which was divided by a copper disc into two sections. The respective parts contained picric acid and sulfuric acid, while the open ends of the tube were sealed with wax. After the acids ate their way through the copper, the resultant chemical mix erupted into flame. The thickness of the disc enabled the maker to vary the time lapse required for a reaction. Thus, the incendiary tube placed on loaded ships would not create a fire until they were well out at sea. Since it would have been difficult, if not impossible, to manufacture the devices in an American plant without detection, an ingenious plan was hatched to make them in the machine shop of a great German liner interned at Hoboken, the *Kaiser Friedrich der Grosse*. Slipping these so-called cigar bombs, alternately known as "pencil bombs," into ships was facilitated by an ample supply of disaffected German and Irish seamen working on American docks. These wicked devices caused any number of cargo fires.

The United States military was so woefully unprepared and undermanned in 1915 that a nation with pretentions as a major power could be called virtually disarmed, and even two years later, when we entered the war, the army's numbers remained sadly lacking while there were no plans in the ready to build forces for a major conflict. The optimist might claim that the nation possessed a modest munitions industry, but it, too, was ill prepared. DuPont continued to control the powder market after the breakup of the powder trust and produced most of the military's smokeless powder, which was the propellant for shells. Then most explosives were produced for industrial and mining use. The government loaded its own shells at military arsenals, either the army's at Picatinny, Morris County, New Jersey, or the navy's Indian Head on the Potomac in Maryland.

Supplying the combatants typically creates opportunities to make significant amounts of money during wartime. Foremost was Bethlehem Steel, founded as an ironworks in 1851, which began producing steel in 1873. In 1885, it opened a plant that made heavy forgings and castings, including forgings for large-caliber guns, and by 1886 it began producing armor plate. The firm's growth was propelled by its military business, and by the early twentieth century, Bethlehem was the largest individual steel company in the United States. Its production included numerous arms and munitions, which at the outbreak of the Great War placed Bethlehem in a good position to become the first American firm to receive a foreign order for armaments. Bethlehem was the only American company that possessed a fully integrated arms business that began with the mining of ore and manufacture of steel, followed by the forging, machining, loading and assembly to a state of completion, for overseas shipment. Bethlehem Steel president Charles Schwab, a visionary in seizing the opportunity of the growing world market for munitions, wasted no time as he visited the Entente powers shortly after the outbreak of war to solicit orders. Schwab's aggressive expansion of the Bethlehem arms business brought enormous profit to the firm and a great expansion of its capacity.[3] However, after the United States sought to enforce new and more restrictive neutrality provisions, a zealous Schwab compromised his country's policy and incurred officials' enmity by shipping parts to Canada for assembly there and export to Britain from Canadian ports. While Bethlehem prospered, this country remained woefully unprepared.

An unidentified, high-ranking army officer attempted to give a sanguine report to the *New York Times* that reflected his hopefulness in the June 6, 1915 headline, "U.S. Can Get Needed Ammunition." After citing our effective production of rifles and cartridges, he noted that "in the matter of artillery we are much less favorably situated. One of the revelations of the present war in Europe has been the overwhelming importance of modern high-power cannon." Not only were they employed in previously unimaginable numbers and effectiveness, but also, as the war progressed, they would consume ammunition in vast, ever-increasing quantities. After the officer cited developments in the explosives field, he urged Congress to move promptly to expand our artillery manufacturing capability and suggested the construction of many military aircraft. Following this country's entry into the war two years later, its munitions capabilities still lagged. The United States was forced to use artillery and airplanes manufactured by its allies, although reasons beyond preparedness contributed to that decision— notably, the need to make effective use of available transport. The Germans possessed an enormous initial weapons advantage because they made their war plans during peacetime.

Gillespie entered the munitions business through the organization of the Union Powder Corporation in 1915, a facility it built in order to supply the Canadian Car and Foundry Company with smokeless powder. It selected a site adjacent to DuPont, a location that appeared to be both sensible and practicable. Ground was broken at Parlin, Sayreville, on May 13 for the plant, which attained a capability to nitrate cotton by July 4. However, Union experienced delays in the delivery of powder presses and mixers, which in turn delayed its powder manufacturing capability until the middle of August. Canadian Car loaded shells for Russia, a combatant that established a physical presence at Parlin by stationing powder inspectors there. Gillespie's first foray into munitions would prove to be short-lived since in October 1915 it sold Union to the Hercules Powder Company, a unit earlier devolved from DuPont. Hercules maintained the operations begun by Gillespie, expanded the plant and retained the original Union name for decades. In retrospect, America's early munitions industry would prove of great benefit as the country drifted into the European war; its experience was invaluable. In addition, after the Russians withdrew from the war, American production for them went to Britain and France. The Raritan River Railroad ran a branch line along the plant and named its terminus at the time Gillespie. This station attained recognition as a minor locality name, a reference still prone to confuse researchers who associate Gillespie with the huge Morgan facility.

Site selection has always been an important factor in the assembling, storage or shipping of munitions. Since it has proved impossible to eliminate the risk of accidental explosion, their separation from populated areas is not only desirable but also essential for public safety. Thus, munitions plants require large tracts of land, which, in view of the economics of the business, should be able to be secured at inexpensive cost. An additional factor in site selection is the desire of industry to minimize potential liability in the event of accident. Choices were often minimal, especially as there was a corresponding need to secure a workforce and enable them to travel to work. Recall that early New Jersey explosives operations were well isolated. The desire to maintain some distance of separation was not always a practical option, however, due to other challenges of transportation, the need for proximity to naval fleets and coastal defense installations. The deadly and dangerous consequences of the storage and handling of explosives in New York had made the public wary for some time.

Two disasters from the recent past loomed in local memory as American industry sought greater flexibility to ship and store its developing munitions business. The earlier one was a February 19, 1903, explosion of an eight-inch shell in a filling room at Fort Lafayette, Brooklyn, that killed about five. This circular brick former coastal defense facility dated from the War of 1812, when it was erected on an artificial island made by cutting off a piece of the Diamond Ledge rock outcropping located near Fort Hamilton. Initially named Fort Diamond, the fort was renamed in honor of the Marquis de Lafayette during his celebrated 1824–25 tour of the United States. After a fire on December 1, 1868, destroyed its interior, although it spared the powder magazine, the fort was used for various munitions functions. The loading of shell there proved a deadly activity. The former fort was destroyed for construction of the Verrazano-Narrows Bridge. Its Brooklyn anchorage rests on the site now.

A routine cargo-handling accident occurred on February 1, 1911, in Jersey City at the Central Railroad docks adjacent to its ferry terminal that is now part of Liberty State Park. It resulted in a powerful blast that was felt fifty miles away, killed at least twenty-four, injured hundreds and reverberated literally and figuratively on both sides of the Hudson. After cases of black powder that were being moved by stevedores exploded, these workers, the loaded lighter, the tug and the ships' crews simply vanished in a blast that rained debris over an extensive area. Panic-stricken New Yorkers ran into downtown streets; glass was broken over much of Lower Manhattan and beyond, a wide area that included the Statue of Liberty. Outraged officials sought criminal charges against those perceived responsible. Demands for more remote and safer handling of explosives impacted the area throughout the war and beyond. The State of New Jersey passed legislation that contained stringent regulations. One proposed remedy was the use of vessels in the harbor as floating magazines. Five years later, the pain and bitterness of lessons not well learned would anger the authorities and alarm an anxious public through another explosion at a nearby location in Jersey City. Oddly, that event, which occurred during the European war, served to remove the 1911 blast from historical consciousness despite its much larger death toll than that of the famed 1916 explosion.

BLACK TOM AND KINGSLAND

An enormous explosion in Jersey City on July 30, 1916, brought the war to the doorstep of the commercial and communication nerve center of the country. An incendiary fire on a barge moored at Black Tom Island, located in the Hudson River near the city's shore in its southern Greenville section, reached its high explosive load about 2:08 a.m. The resultant blast rocked New York City, was felt nearly one hundred miles away and seared the consciousness of the nation. The death toll of only about six was overshadowed by property damage estimated at $20 million. An investigation to determine the cause was undertaken immediately. At first, accident was suspected, but after this initial belief was replaced by sabotage, a wary public was stunned by the dismal realization that the European war was now on our shores. Broken glass littered the streets of New York. In an era when insurance companies specialized in a single line of coverage, the plate glass insurance industry was figuratively shattered. Flying fragments damaged the Statue of Liberty. Vessels in the harbor rocked at their moorings, including a quarantine ship, while fireboats pulled other ships out of harm's way. Their rescues included a four-masted schooner with its sails shot away. Raining ordnance imperiled the boats' firemen crews.

A massive explosion at Black Tom Island in Jersey City caused few deaths, but property damage was extensive and awesome. The blast instilled fear in the populace as it brought a then European war to the shores of New York. Two results were heightened security and new explosives-handling regulations in the Port of New York.

Devastation and destruction were spread across the Black Tom facility. Some huge warehouses were turned into piles of smoldering ruin, while others simply disappeared. The *Times* claimed no vestige remained of the National Storage Company warehouses nearest the explosion, "not a brick or mark where they stood—only black holes in the ground and blackened ends of broken piers pointing like death fingers through the debris-littered surface of the harbor." Wrecked barges and railway cars littered the area. Fate intervened with a helping hand. The death toll was kept low by the miraculous escapes of many.

The role of the island of Black Tom in the history of Jersey City was both odious and odiferous. There is local claim that the attribution of the Black Tom name is for an early African American fisherman dweller. However, this appears to be folklore considering that mid-nineteenth-century guides for anglers referred to the place as a big "rock." The nearby railroads sought to extend their waterfront property into the harbor to connect with Black Tom, which was regarded as an odious presumption. The *Times* said of the place on July 27, 1869, "A little body of earth shooting above the surface of the water forms the nucleus of the island of larger dimensions which the Central Railroad has made it into." Their focus was the form of the fill, the stinking offal of New York. The content was not the city's street sweepings, which had an agricultural market as fertilizer, but rotting garbage of sundry sort consisting of decaying vegetable and animal matter, including "the bodies of dead dogs, cats, etc." The putrid landfill was not the only occasion that brought Black Tom into public attention during the era. Following a powder factory explosion there on January 16, 1875, the resulting fire burned four workers to a crisp.[4]

The early suspicions of incendiarism were confirmed by the report of an investigation by Colonel Beverley W. Dunn, a West Point graduate and retired artillery officer and then head of the American Railway Association's Bureau of Explosives, which was released in May 1917. Dunn's findings were directed to transportation issues, notably the need for the prompt loading of vessels in the harbor to reduce the quantities of explosives stored on docks and in rail yards. A reporter admitted that the findings might not be helpful as the authorities searched for the perpetrators. Two decades would pass before responsibility was conclusively placed on German subversives.

The second major blow by saboteurs in New Jersey was the destruction of the Kingsland (Lyndhurst) plant of the Canadian Car and Foundry Company. Its factory was built in 1916 in the vast swamp that spanned much of southern Bergen and western Hudson Counties. Appreciation that would later be afforded natural wet environments served to give the area new respect and, as a consequence, its renaming as the Meadowlands. The aforementioned firm, headquartered in Montreal, was a major supplier of loaded shells to British and Russian forces. The conspiracy to destroy the plant was facilitated by an operative who secured a job in Canadian's personnel department, a position that enabled him to hire other infiltrators. One, a plant hand named Theodore Wuzniak, set a fire at his workstation, which, once it reached explosives, began a series of massive blasts that destroyed the plant. The regular and frequent eruptions motivated a heroine, telephone operator Theresa Louise McNamara, who stayed at her switchboard as the fire intensified and contacted each building with a warning to flee. Her courageous action was recognized at the time by the National Special Aid Society and later by the Lyndhurst Historical Society, which dedicated a vest pocket park to her memory. Remarkably, no one was killed. The Kingsland blast set off panic at the nearby County of Hudson institutions, which included a hospital for the insane, an almshouse and a penitentiary, located at Snake Hill, an outcropping of the Palisades, about three miles from the plant. Exertions by the staff were needed to quell fears of impending doom among the fearful inmates.

While the focus of this book is high explosives, it's worth noting that the DuPont smokeless powder operation was also struck by major explosions. In New Jersey, a blast at Carneys Point on the Delaware River on January 10, 1916, killed five, while an explosion on January 13, 1917, at Haskell in Passaic County was felt in four states. An obscure, short-lived American Smokeless Powder Association operation established near the future Gillespie grounds exploded in December 1916, killing one.

War workers themselves were potential targets of saboteurs, a risk experienced by the hundred or so who, on July 31, 1915, were riding on a Raritan River Railroad express train that regularly carried munitions workers from Metuchen to the DuPont and Union Powder plants in Parlin. Spikes that were left on the rails, in all likelihood by saboteurs, were successful in causing a derailment. While four were injured and a score shaken up, the potential disaster put all of them at risk. The *Times* reported the next day that over five thousand persons were engaged in munitions manufacture in Middlesex County, which created a multitude of local targets. The aforementioned plants, which employed three thousand of them, had one hundred armed guards for protection.

Preventing these attacks proved difficult, in part because a mere century ago no federal counterintelligence operation existed, a realization

The 1915 derailment of a Raritan River Railroad train that carried war industry workers demonstrated that sabotage was not limited to factories.

inconceivable in the post-9/11 world. In the later nineteenth century, the military abandoned its intelligence operations undertaken after the Civil War. Thus, military intelligence was left to a wartime operator, Allan Pinkerton, who founded a private detective service, the Pinkerton Agency, which, along with others of the type, performed government security work. Admittedly, labor agitation rather than alien spying was paramount among the government's interests. A Bureau of Investigation was formed in 1908 after Congress barred Secret Service personnel from detective work, but still, at the time no federal statute made espionage or sabotage during peacetime a crime. The attorney general proposed legislation in 1916 that would have made such activity an offense, but only after America declared war was the Espionage Act of 1917 passed. The scenario is a striking contrast to the early twenty-first century, when the military, federal civilian law enforcement and foreign intelligence appear to compete with one another, each seeming to exercise desires to extend their respective authority beyond traditional legal bounds. In the early twenty-first century, even a municipality, the City of New York, has a counter-terrorism unit. At the outset of the Great War, the lack of intelligence not only facilitated the work of saboteurs but also made investigation and detection of their deeds difficult.

The lack of any national control over explosives was not only another of American's war preparedness shortcomings but also a condition where the "uncontrolled production and possession of explosives obviously became a serious menace to the safety of persons and property and the successful conduct of military operations."[5] This security flaw was addressed by the Federal Explosives Act of 1917, which permitted the federal government to assume powers that may have belonged to the states, an action justified by military necessity. The foreword to the act leaves no doubt that its controls were directed primarily at saboteurs: "Our enemies are not all in Europe, and it was a weapon to be turned against those of them who are lurking here on our own soil that this law was created."[6] Although the act addressed a wartime exigency, the government ascertained that the Bureau of Mines of the Department of the Interior was the agency best able to assume immediate oversight of the law's strictures. The bureau, itself formed only in 1910, was organized to exercise supervision of explosives in mines, whereas in peacetime 80 percent of domestic consumption was expended. War Department knowledge of every source of explosives was needed to guard against explosives falling into the hands of enemy operatives, including domestic saboteurs.

The steep decline in the activity of enemy agents that followed the United States' entry into the war was a consequence perhaps not to have been unexpected. Despite the Germans' heightened need to destroy America's war-making capacity, that aspiration was offset by the increased risk to their operatives if captured—namely, death. Sabotage during wartime is a capital offense, and this proved a major disincentive for the sundry would-be saboteurs, many of whom sought safety through furtive escapes to Mexico. The risk of years of confinement if caught was one thing for an enemy operative, but it was quite another to put his neck on the line.

One major incident occurred shortly after America entered the war. Admittedly, advance planning rather than chance was the likely cause of the nation's heaviest death toll from explosion during World War I. The blast at Eddystone, Pennsylvania, near Chester occurred only six days after the April 4 declaration of war, so it is believed that the plans were made beforehand. The Eddystone Ammunition Corporation employed many young women. About 380 workers were filling shrapnel shells for the Russian government in Building F on the morning of the tenth when three blasts, including a major first eruption at about 9:55 a.m. followed by two lesser ones, leveled the building. Most of the 132 killed were women; many were never identified. Strong suspicions of sabotage pointed to varied sources, but some of the suggested plots were preposterous, and none was definitively proved.

With respect to American industry, the Central Intelligence Agency revealed that from early 1915 through the spring of 1917, forty-three factories were plagued by explosions or suspicious fire. Some were prominent, such as the John A. Roebling wire manufacturing plant in Trenton, where a New Year's Day 1915 incendiary fire broke out. However, the possibility of sabotage does not appear in the firm's history. Many others were not well known. Four dozen ships incurred mysterious fires. As was noted, the exertions of the plotters were not impeded by any statute specifically forbidding peacetime sabotage or espionage. The authorities were handicapped by a requirement to detect, record and prosecute saboteurs for other offences.

The nefarious activities of saboteurs extended beyond the usual instruments of war. The old adage that "an army marches on its stomach" is reality, not a cliché. Food rationing instituted during the world wars was to ensure that fighting forces were well fed. Conversely, denying your enemy food diminishes his fighting capability. Thus, as retribution for starvation caused at home by the British naval blockade, the Germans undertook a campaign to destroy American food supplies. Its effectiveness was brought to light by the *New York Times* on November 3, 1917, under the headline: "Germans Here Burn Millions in Food." The article enumerated major losses and claimed that destruction caused by the incendiary fires experienced since the country declared war was equal to a year's rations for 300,000 men. The insurance industry took note that there was an active ongoing fire prevention campaign, reinforcing the charge with statistics and likely cases. Food facilities were not as well protected as arms plants, so they were often easy targets. Horses, too, were targeted by saboteurs. A firebug attempted to set afire a corral of eight to nine hundred of them at the West Shore Railroad's freight yards in Weehawken as they awaited shipment to England and France, according to an account in the *New York Times* of November 17, 1915.

Analysis of the American declaration of war and its timing, which has been ongoing for nearly a century and will be the subject of new scholarship as the war's centennial approaches, will not be reiterated here. However, insight can be gained by realizing the major matters then on American minds. First, submarine warfare, which many feared as a weapon of terror, took a heavy toll on American lives, materials and ships. The loss of the aforementioned *Lusitania* shocked the sensibilities of a country that was unaware that the passenger liner was also a floating arsenal. Second,

General John J. Pershing, pictured in an uncharacteristic smiling pose, delayed deployment of American forces until they were able to operate as an independent fighting unit. *Courtesy of Robert A. Schoeffling.*

a British propaganda campaign that began following the alleged Belgian atrocities and accelerated after the *Lusitania*, which demonized the German fighter as subhuman, had tremendous influence in America. On the other hand, the British did not always uphold the rules of war by arming under disguise merchant ships, and much of their "public relations" campaign consisted of lies. Third, American bankers and industrialists had investments of staggering sums that would be at risk it the Entente was not victorious. President Woodrow Wilson was narrowly reelected in 1916 by a margin of victory no doubt ensured by his campaign's reminder that he kept us out of war. His March 5, 1917 second inaugural address sought unity, upheld

The World War I Middlesex Munitions Disaster

American values and offered a faint prospect for peace. A month later, with our future allies alienated by his protracted delay, Wilson asked Congress for a declaration of war, which was promptly passed, although not without dissent and with a number of "yeas" given begrudgingly. (Hereafter, the Entente is referred to as the Allies.) General John J. Pershing was appointed commander of the American forces. Much of America was unaware what war would entail. The clueless did not realize we would need to raise a large army. The hopeful thought we could build this force through volunteers. The wary did not believe there would be available shipping to send them to Europe. After the arrival of the first units in France, months would be spent training and awaiting additional manpower to enable the Americans to operate as separate units.

4

BUILDING AMERICA'S MUNITIONS INDUSTRY

Arming and supplying an American fighting force of unprecedented size and might necessitated a massive transformation of American military and industrial production. In retrospect, the construction of shell-loading plants would be one of the country's finest achievements. However, not only were the anticipated needs cited in the previous chapter not fulfilled, but even America's entry in the war could not sufficiently speed production. The war began with only eighty-seven commissioned personnel in the Ordnance Department.[1] Some of the army men were ill clothed while stateside during the winter of 1916–17. During the testimony of Samuel Matthews Vauclain, the chairman of the production committee of the Council of National Defense, before the Committee on Military Affairs of the United States Senate on December 18, 1917, Senator Kenneth McKellar of Tennessee grumbled that after a congressional appropriation of $12 million for machine guns on August 29, 1916, nothing had been accomplished on the subject by June 7 or 8 of 1917. It took a long time to decide on what particular gun. While the chairman of the War Industries Board gave priority to ordering shells, Vauclain pointed out that the proper precedence for production would be to ensure the availability of needed powder and gun carriages, which took much longer to produce. General William Crozier informed the Senate that not only does it take a year to make artillery, but also gun carriage and equipment contracts were by necessity given to firms with no prior experience, which required additional (wasted) time for drawings and related details.[2]

The World War I Middlesex Munitions Disaster

Visionary Crozier (1855–1942), United States Military Academy 1876, organized the Ordnance Department for emergency service in the field well prior to the United States' entry in the war. He was an early advocate for industrial preparedness by his recognition of the interdependence of ordnance with civilian science, engineering and industry.[3] In short, the magnitude of the situation was so great that after the war, Benedict Crowell, the assistant secretary of war, director of munitions, could write, "On April 6, 1917, the United States scarcely realized the gravity of the undertaking."[4]

Munitions requirements would be in quantities far beyond the scope of what United States government producers ever imagined, let alone manufactured, and they would be needed quickly. The capacity of the American plants that were producing for the Allies was a small fraction of what was required. The need was perceived, however, making Senator James W. Wadsworth Jr. of New York prescient for his observation, "The side which will bring to bear the greatest numbers in guns and men, which are all dependent upon organized industries, will eventually wear out and subdue the other side."[5]

As background to the shell-loading story, the United States' entry into the war in April 1917 immediately brought a change in the country's planning for munitions production by cooperation with the Allies and the establishment of an Interallied Munitions Pool. In the evaluation of respective capabilities, it was recognized "that the Allies had a surplus of machining capacity but needed explosives, raw materials and semi-finished products, while America lacked present machining capacity but was able to supply the very things the Allies needed. The condition made team work as advantageous in industrial, as it was imperative in military operations." The emerging practice would have all materials go into a "common pot" to serve all, and as a consequence the "Allies provided the American forces with artillery and its ammunition, and in effect they equipped the first divisions with nearly everything save their rifles and small-arms ammunition. America provided the Allies with a considerable part of their propellants and explosives, sent them more than two gun forgings for every finished gun purchased abroad, and sent a variety of semi-finished material for final treatment abroad." From a balance of payments standpoint, after the war it was calculated that for every dollar America spent abroad for material, the Allies spent five dollars here for munitions.[6] Another exigency was crucial to this planning—a critical shortage of shipping capacity. The smaller bulk of American raw materials expanded the effective cargo capacity of the strained merchant marines.

An explanation by Crowell of how shells explode and the loading process will add clarity to the text that follows. There are two classes of military explosives: the propellants, usually smokeless powder, and high explosives, which provide the destructive force. The detonation of a high explosive shell, actually a series of explosions, occurs thusly:

> *The firing pin strikes the percussion primer, which explodes the detonator. The detonator is filled with some easily detonated substance, such as fulminate of mercury. The concussion of this explosion sets off the charge held within the long tube which extends down the middle of the shell and which is known as the booster. The booster charge is a substance easily exploded, such as tetryl or trinitroaniline (T.N.A.) The explosion of the booster jars off the main charge of the shell, T.N.T., or amatol. This system of detonator, booster, and main charge gives control of the explosive within the shell, safety in the handling of the shell and complete explosion when the shell bursts.*

A shell-loading plant assembles and loads field artillery ammunition made up of a steel projectile loaded with a bursting charge. Trinitrotoluol, commonly abbreviated as TNT, was the bursting charge early in the war but was later usually replaced by amatol. The projectile is exploded upon impact by a percussion fuse, which discharges a sensitive detonator or boosting charge of tetryl, which in turn detonates the TNT charge. This is "fixed" ammunition in which the projectile and propellant are assembled into a unit. By comparison, heavy guns have their projectile and propelling charges loaded separately. In fixed ammunition, the projectile is placed on a brass cartridge case, in which is inserted an appropriate quantity of smokeless powder. This is the propellant that is exploded by a percussion or electrical primer, which provides the means of throwing or delivering the projectile. The whole is not unlike an ordinary brass pistol cartridge, although on a very large scale.[7]

After the military realized early in the war that sufficient supplies of TNT could not be produced, the Americans switched to amatol, a British explosive innovation. Amatol is a mixture of ammonium nitrate and trinitrotoluene, usually in proportions of 80/20 or 50/50 with the first figure the number of parts of ammonium nitrate and the second the parts of TNT. The finding of and at times creating new sources of raw materials, including nitrate, is an additional chapter of American munitions success but beyond the ambit of this work. The ammonium nitrate is mixed and heated with TNT preparatory to the amatol's passing into shells.[8]

The World War I Middlesex Munitions Disaster

In World War I, when artillery became the predominant killer, five massive plants were planned to furnish the shells for America's contribution. The first of them was privately built adjacent to Hercules at Parlin, Sayreville, not far distant from the Gillespie future site. Four others were built later for the government; three of these nearly identical enormous loading facilities were located in New Jersey. The exigencies of war brought opportunities for the smaller operators that had attained experience in shell loading by supplying the Entente. Prior to the world war, the American military's modest need for shell was met by the aforementioned government arsenals.

Joseph D. Evans, a 1901 graduate of the Massachusetts Institute of Technology, was a prime beneficiary as the sudden need for an expanded munitions industry war elevated his significance and role. When Evans sought a commission at the outset of the United States' entry into the war, he was told that since he was one of four men in the country with shell-loading experience, his contribution to the war effort would be greater in the manufacturing sphere. Evans had been an effective, experienced engineer who operated the destroyed Kingsland plant, so the United States Ordnance Department awarded a contract to the J.D. Evans Engineering Company for loading three-inch and 75mm shells. This was evidently the first of the major plants, as inferred by its early commencement of construction in July 1917. The Thomas A. Gillespie Company served as general contractor. The plant was ready to operate on October 15 but did not load shells until November 14 due to unavailable components. No complete rounds were produced until January 1, 1918, due to the lack of detonating fuses, but Evans was expected to reach a daily capacity of thirty thousand shells.

Evans was either linked with a second local firm, the California Loading Company, or its operations were intertwined. Industrial directories described California as a manufacturer of detonating fuses, boosters and hand grenades. Both firms were given an Old Bridge location, an imprecise place name that should not be mistaken for the present township of Old Bridge, a municipality that, until 1975, had been known as Madison Township. Old Bridge in the context of neighborhood or section was a locality near the confluence of three municipalities, including the former Madison Township, the township of East Brunswick and the borough of Sayreville. While each claimed a part of historic Old Bridge, the present historic district of Old Bridge is in East Brunswick Township. The Evans/California plant appears to have been in southwest Sayreville, adjoining Bordentown Avenue on a site that is now, in part, occupied by the Sayreville recycling center.

Some remains of Gillespie's nearby California Loading plant are located on the grounds of the Sayreville recycling center on Bordentown Avenue.

These brief remarks about Evans underscore a critical challenge of World War I ordnance production and a hazard for uncovering their history. The Ordnance Department faced an enormous task planning and delivering the needed components to facilitate the completion of loaded shell. The historian can detect that many firms were active in the period, but their operations are buried in obscurity. The thirty thousand daily capacity of Evans's shell production, a figure reflected in government reports, means this was a very large plant. Nearly all the other information on Evans is found in an informational report that was self-published in 1919 by J.D. Evans Engineering Company, *Report of the Old Bridge Shell Loading Plant*, which is quoted in the National Register nomination of the *Bethlehem Loading Company Mays Landing Plant Archeological Historic District* written by Joan Berkey. The paper trail of the Gillespie plant will be little better, but first look briefly at the other government plants.

All of these plants required enormous tracts that could be acquired inexpensively, a truism for munitions operations. They needed locations away from settled areas, a buffer from their surroundings and access to transport, both to receive raw materials and to ship loaded shell. Water facilities were preferred for outgoing shipping. Morgan would build on-site

The World War I Middlesex Munitions Disaster

The plants included dormitories for workers who chose to live on site. This living area, typical of the type, is from the Gillespie affiliate, California Loading plant, located nearby in Sayreville.

employee residential facilities, but the two other government plants in New Jersey also constructed accompanying new towns.

DuPont built the large loading plant located outside New Jersey, in Pennimen, Virginia, but note must also be taken of the singular accomplishment of the firm's other numerous and major contributions to the war effort, especially that of the construction of the largest smokeless powder manufactory the world had ever seen. The plant near Nashville, Tennessee, named Old Hickory because it was located not far from the home of President Andrew Jackson, was built in record time after the laying of seven miles of railroad required to transport building materials to the site. There, "production of sulfuric acid began sixty-seven days after ground-breaking, nitric acid nine days later, guncotton, the raw material of smokeless powder, two weeks after that. The first finished powder was granulated 116 days after the breaking of ground for the plant, 121 days ahead of contract agreement." While DuPont made a 1 percent profit on the value of production, their charge to the government for construction was a symbolic single dollar.[9]

A staff of thirty thousand male and female workers had to be located wherever they could be found, trained and housed in a town of 3,867 buildings, a number in addition to the 1,112 that composed the plant. After the rail line was double-tracked, each day it handled 1,100 cars and thirty-one thousand passengers.[10]

The Pennimen plant, also a feat of rapid construction, occupied 5,114 acres in an isolated area that required a new town to house workers. After construction began on March 1, 1918, production commenced on June 20 for this operation that both manufactured boosters and loaded shells of four sizes. The warm Virginia weather caused early difficulty with amatol, a problem that was later overcome. A labor shortage led to the use of military personnel at the Pennimen plant.[11]

Bethlehem Steel Company, already extensively engaged in armaments industries, was a logical choice to build one of the huge plants and was chosen to erect a facility in southern New Jersey. Bethlehem bought eighteen thousand acres along the Great Egg Harbor and South Rivers in Atlantic County near Mays Landing. Much of it was poor-quality, sandy, swampy or heavily wooded land. The parts with the greater utility value were chosen for the shell-loading plant to be operated by their subsidiary, the Bethlehem Loading Company, and a town to house its workers. The firm was known by the acronym Belco, while the town was Belcoville. The isolated area required a new rail line to bring in construction materials and everything else. Two bridges and a three-hundred-car classification yard were built to support the rail operation.

> *The first lumber for the plant program was received on the 3rd of April, and by the middle of August there stood a complete town that would house about 400 families and 3,000 single people…Streets and sidewalks were laid out, sewage system, water system an electric lighting system installed, and later, heating plants for heating dwellings and all buildings installed… But little behind was the construction of the plant buildings, powerhouse and storage buildings. Here eleven units, each unit consisting of a receiving building, a crushing, drying, melting, mixing and extruding building, and a finishing building were erected for the loading of the shell with a total producing capacity of 25,000 75mm, 12,000 155 mm and 4,000 8-inch or larger shell per day…Ground was broken about the middle of April and such rapid progress was made in the construction and the equipment that the first 155 mm shell was loaded on July 1, 1918.*

Also built at Belco were the necessary magazines, storage facilities, powerhouse and ancillary structures.[12]

Joseph D. Evans's enhanced stature was reflected by his crucial role in another of the major loading plants. He was appointed the production vice-president and key operations officer of the second Atlantic County plant,

The activity of these shell-loading workers is not specified, but the scene is not a standard production line.

the Atlantic Loading Company, a group controlled by New York investors. Located at Hammonton, Atlantic's plant, informally named Amatol for the new explosive material, was rapidly built in an isolated area that also required an accompanying town. The firm purchased six thousand acres of mostly wooded, with some acres of swampy, land located about twenty-five miles northwest of Atlantic City. The western border was about four miles east of Hammonton, while the tract was adjacent on the north to the Pennsylvania and Reading Railroads. After the clearance of dense, tangled growth, the fast-track construction project, which began on March 4, 1918, built an average of four buildings per day, some going up almost overnight. Amatol began loading operations on July 31, 1918, and completed its first rounds of 75mm shells three days later. The plant claimed a safety innovation, the use of water-jacketed rather than steam heating kettles, and a production first, belt conveyors. The 350-acre town, which was located two miles away, included recreational, entertainment and commercial facilities that permitted a self-contained lifestyle. The Amatol plant was not yet complete at the armistice. This facility is well documented through a book-length report published by Atlantic Loading that detailed its construction and operation. It was accessible online at publication.[13] A perspective different

The French were esteemed as the world's premier artillerists. The 75mm was the war's most potent weapon. *Courtesy of Robert A. Schoeffling.*

from the glowing firm-produced history was put forward by the government. Hunter indicated that at this plant, which was designed to load four different shells and manufacture boosters, considerable difficulty was met with both construction and operation, so only 75mm shell had been produced at the time of the armistice.[14]

Prior to the Gillespie plant at Morgan, recall that Thomas A. Gillespie had earlier manufactured munitions in Sayreville for the Entente powers (see Chapter 3). Gillespie operated the plant at Parlin for only a short period before its sale to Hercules. However, he possessed a number of qualities that made him a worthy choice for the Morgan site. Gillespie had engineering acumen, a proven ability to establish and oversee systems for the moving of materials and manufacturing experience with multiple products. He had the ability to oversee exacting requirements for filling shells and the capability to organize and operate this factory operation. One account suggests that Morgan may have been a second choice.

The background of the Morgan site and its earlier consideration for military use is also of interest as some of the eventual plant grounds, along with a region around Cheesequake Creek, were contemplated for a function allied to munitions—a proving ground. The government was offered part of the eventual Gillespie location in 1891, when D. Noble Rowan proposed selling an L-shaped tract that had a frontage measuring less than a mile on Raritan Bay and which extended back about a mile perpendicular to it. The report continued, "The portion near the shore, and lying between it and the New York and Long Branch Railroad, consists of a plateau nearly a half mile long and three-eighths of a mile wide, overlooking the remainder of the land and well suited to the location of batteries for firing inland or to sea." The report referred to the tract as Morgan, but one can infer from the plot's description that much of the land was in Old Bridge, as it was "north of the section in Cheesequake Creek, on the banks of which extends a salt marsh 8 or 9 miles back into the country and from 2–5 miles wide." However, there followed two practical issues that made it understandable why the proposal was not consummated. First, the government candidly admitted that "this marsh could not cheaply be drained," which is a plain realization of the long-existing character of the Cheesequake Creek region. Second, there was the substantial cost of the land, estimated at $1 million. In addition, and just as important, was the terrain's lack of suitability for a proving ground firing range. The soft, marshy character of the land would have made it difficult to locate tested ordnance. There was also a claim that suggested that Morgan might have been a second choice for the loading plant.

Alpern & Company, one of Middlesex County's leading real estate brokers, claimed in 1917 a role in the war preparation effort by securing land for four area munitions plants. The firm regarded its efforts for Morgan as a special coup and asserted that it persuaded the government to relocate here a loading plant that was ostensibly planned for along the Ohio River in Pittsburgh.[15] The same report indicated that price was the convincing factor, as some local land was acquired in the range of twenty to thirty dollars per acre. The firm's boastful account cannot be verified, but the nature of much of the territory, spent clay fields and marsh, can lend credence to their claims of cost effectiveness. The skeptic may infer, however, that proximity to the Atlantic was the overriding consideration for Morgan, even if there had been an alternate site. Cheesequake Creek ran through the tract, a waterway once important for local navigation, notably to the former Cheesequake section of Old Bridge Township. The stream is the border with Sayreville at this point, which obviously made the southern expanse of the plant located in Old Bridge Township. More importantly, this waterway was needed as the outlet for barges or lighters that carried loaded shell, a factor perhaps even more significant than cost in site selection. Since the broking of munitions property may not have enhanced the firm's reputation after the explosion, Isaac Alpern's vanity biography in volume three of Wall's *History of Middlesex County, 1664–1920* omits this phase of his business background.

Various figures have been cited to describe the area of the plant. Its acquisition, along with other purchasing decisions, was facilitated by the Thomas A. Gillespie Company having been given the status as agent for the government. This arrangement provided a legal standing that enabled quick decision-making and fast transactions, as they could avoid delays by circumventing the details of procurement regulations. The plant property was bought in the name of the Gillespie firm with the proviso that it would be turned over to the government at the appropriate time. The actual acreage, variously listed as different numbers, may not be determinable, although locating the survey of the grounds might help. The plant was acquired in six tracts; some are described with numerous courses and contain prior exceptions from the described plots. Some parts of the grounds were leased, which complicates area determination as that type of transaction has no need to be recorded and typically does not contain a survey. A figure cited in official reports is 2,200 acres. The 1994 Archives Search Report indicated 3,880 acres, but it may have included the area the army inspected outside the plant grounds. The best description of the owned section is probably the transaction where the Thomas A. Gillespie Loading Company conveyed the grounds to the United States of America on June 10, 1921, which can be found in *Middlesex Deeds*, Book 698, although it does not reference total acreage.

The Morgan grounds had the advantage of an extensive, inexpensive property, but it was closer to settlement than would ordinarily be desired. The plant would erect numerous residential and dormitory structures, but an accompanying town would not be required. In addition, available rail and trolley facilities would enable a workforce to be drawn from along the lines' routes. However, proximity to a population was a sensitive public relations issue and often had a negative impact. The army's reservations were revealed by Lieutenant Colonel R.H. Hawkins in his August 20, 1919 testimony on war expenditures. He told that a loading plant that was expected to be built near Camp Dix, New Jersey, was moved because the camp's commanding officer said he did not want it near his soldiers.[16]

The New Year at Morgan began with the January 2 start of construction of the Gillespie plant. Reports of progress are limited to a few minor news items, which unfortunately are the only surviving details about construction of the Morgan plant. However, since the four shell-loading facilities that were built simultaneously were nearly identical, clearer understanding of the layout and function of the loading operation can be garnered from descriptions of the Atlantic Loading Company and the Bethlehem Loading Company plants, together with the Gillespie plot plan. The British, who had a two-years-plus head start in high-volume loading and had mastered production systems earlier in the war, aided the American efforts. At the request of the United States government, they sent Major H.L. Armstrong and Dr. T. Martin Lowry to oversee the construction of our new installations. They are key figures to the American munitions operation, but little is known about them. Gillespie's contract with the government recompensed him for costs plus 10 percent. The cost of the plant, based on imprecise, only somewhat reliable amounts cited after the explosion, was $18 million, which using the value of the dollar in late 2012 was the equivalent of about $300 million.

The Gillespie buildings were, for the most part, one-story frame construction over concrete floors. The wall and roof cladding was galvanized steel. Loading buildings were two stories, with the upper floor utilized for melting and mixing rooms located above the pouring rooms. These buildings included brick firewalls, which extended down to the first floor and separated the melting kettles. This safety measure was installed to reduce the risk from this relatively hazardous operation. An empty room placed adjacent to the kettle room was used for temporary storage of amatol waste or scrap. Firewalls also separated the loading room.

TNT storage and service magazines, each planned to hold 150,000 pounds, were of similar construction. They were surrounded by timber earth-filled bulkheads four feet wide at the top and six to ten feet wide at the base, a construction design intended to contain an explosion at any one.

The ammonium nitrate buildings, fifty by three hundred feet, had brick foundations and brick walls to a height of eight feet, while their floors were also concrete. Warehouses for components and completed rounds were wood frame over wood floors with corrugated galvanized iron cladding. Their dimensions were fifty by five hundred, excepting one that was one thousand feet long. It was divided by a firewall.

The power plant produced steam for production power. It survived the explosion and fire. A fragment of a wall is still standing.

The World War I Middlesex Munitions Disaster

The loading school for inspectors at Morgan was a broadly organized enterprise, the plant comprising three school buildings, erected on a six acre plot. Two of these buildings were two-story barracks, each with accommodations for thirty-two students. The third was the school building proper... The faculty staff comprised five instructors, four of them graduates of the school. The first class graduated June 8, 1918.[17]

The utilization of skilled, effective inspectors would prove to be the most critical aspect of shell-loading employment.

The temporary nature of the buildings not only permitted cost savings upward of 50 percent but also shortened construction time. Atlantic utilized fabricated steel assembled in panels at the factory, a technique that was probably also utilized at the companion plants. These bolted units could be readily disassembled and reused, thus enhancing their potential salvage value.

Fire halted progress on February 18, a blaze that destroyed a twenty-five-by one-hundred-foot building. While there was little value in the temporary frame and corrugated steel structure itself—it was typical of the shell-loading type—greater loss was incurred by the destruction of its contents of plumbing supplies and equipment. Construction work quickly resumed over this vast site, a place that caught the attention of a curious public. The place became a local tourist attraction, one that drew thousands of visitors every Sunday. People were captivated, for example, of one day's parade of 518 teams (of horses with wagons) that entered the massive undertaking, according to one observer with a penchant for detail. In time, the plant was enclosed for reasons of safety and security. After it was, the seventeen miles of fence required became a measure of its vastness. While this number was reported in the news, it seems rather high; a later indication of eight miles appears more reliable.

The *Times* criticized the layout of the plant after the explosion, claiming on October 6 that

the plan under which the great collection of buildings composing the Gillespie plant were built of wood and placed in such relation that the destruction of one building meant the destruction of all was devised by the Ordnance Department. Under this plan it was found possible to break all records in the almost magical erection of a vast plant, while the production achieved at the newly-made plant in three months was considered to be one of the greatest industrial feats of the war. The purpose of the great concentration

53

of explosives in one group of buildings was the superior efficiency expected from so vast an enterprise and before yesterday the plan had justified the hopes placed in it.

This quotation is contrary to what many, certainly those in the vicinity who shared the personal risk of a disaster, would have expected. In addition, this plan defies the most elementary principles of risk management and loss control.

Each plant employed an architect. Since these practitioners were working with a substantially common design, the on-site architect's responsibilities were for the most part construction supervision, along with miscellaneous design work for the inevitable additions and alterations. Joseph Swannell, the Gillespie architect, was born in Brooklyn in 1858 and moved with his family while a youngster to Red Bank, where his father, Thomas, a Civil War veteran, was a builder. While Joseph early in his career worked for his father and as a cabinetmaker, he also studied architecture. He opened a Red Bank office in 1891. Swannell's many local commissions include two admired public buildings: St. James Roman Catholic Church and the Red Bank Armory.

The younger Swannell also followed a military career by joining the Red Bank Calvary Troop as a charter member. In 1916, when he held the rank of lieutenant, Swannell left with them for service in the Mexican War. His employment at Gillespie was punctured by the singularly sad experience of learning of the loss of his only son in the Great War. Thomas Burton Swannell, known as Burton, was killed in action in France just one week before the Gillespie plant was destroyed.

Each unit of the respective plants was equipped to make a particular weapon, typically the loading of a certain size shell. Each operation was centered along a row of three key functioning structures, which had long and relatively narrow footprints and which, together with ancillary buildings, completed the unit. Empty shells were stored in a building adjacent to the loading building, which was often two stories, where blending, mixing and heating of the explosives, usually amatol, was done on the upper story prior to this heated, molten mixture being sent to the filling room below. The loaded shell was then capped, finished, cleaned, shellacked, marked and packed prior to moving to the loaded shell building. Shells, packed in wood crates, usually left the plant by lighter along Cheesequake Creek for transfer to ships in Sandy Hook Bay. The strict regulations that governed the movement of explosives in New York Harbor constrained handling and shipping. A "shell

The major shell-loading plants were built to a common basic plan, but each had an architect on staff. Joseph Swannell of Red Bank served at Gillespie. *Courtesy of Dorn's Classic Images.*

hospital" was given over to working out problems with shells that did not pass inspection. Other buildings in a unit stored each type of material in a separate structure and provided accommodations for employees.

The unit that eventually exploded, 6-1-1, was the first to be completed at the end of May when experimental loading of shell began. Actual production commenced on June 12 and was continuous up to the time of the accident. As it became apparent that the coordination of the receipt of incoming component parts and outgoing shipping would be problems, the number of storage facilities at the plant was ordered increased.

The potential risk to the surrounding area created by the presence of the plant prompted some local activists to advocate for preparedness. They urged that a home defense league be established, one preferably based in South Amboy. The need and urgency were pointed out in an anonymous letter to the *South Amboy Citizen*, which claimed that South Amboy, already a major shipper of munitions and coal, would soon be surrounded by twenty to thirty thousand war workers. Following the completion of the Gillespie plant, the region would be "practically the center of the national defense."

A companion advertisement speculated in print by wondering if such a preparedness organization would be formed only after the city experienced disasters in the magnitude of the aforementioned Eddystone and Kingsland explosions or a suspicious fire not unlike the one that occurred the prior month at Port Newark, or even a catastrophe comparable to Halifax.

PORT NEWARK AND HALIFAX

The two latter events merit close examination because they provide insight into the area's mood at the time. Port Newark suggested the potential for disruption of the nation's war machine, while Halifax was horrendous proof that an accidental explosion had a theretofore unimaginable potential for widespread catastrophic destruction. Fears of enemy saboteurs spread through the Newark area after the uncovering of a sabotage plot in early January 1918. The public became alarmed over incendiarism following a January 26 fire of four oil barges located at Port Newark near the 4,500-foot U.S. Navy pier. The rapidly spreading blaze destroyed the pier, threatened an extensive complex of buildings of the U.S Quartermaster Corps and imperiled the nearby Submarine Boat Corporation, which had planned to construct 150 ships. Firemen battled the flames for twelve hours before the fire was under control. Their exertions included wetting nearby buildings to help halt the fire's spread. Reports that suspicious figures had been in the area elevated the wariness of both the public and the authorities. Armed private citizens were quickly deputized to guard the area but were soon replaced by soldiers. The revelation three weeks later that the fire was caused by the negligence of a contractor on the site provided only partial relief of local anxiety. Residents were again fearful on February 9, when fire destroyed both a Lehigh Valley Railroad depot located about a mile from the pier and many loaded freight cars. The cause of this fire has never been determined. However, the terror in Newark paled in comparison to Halifax's experience a scant few weeks earlier.

On December 6, 1917, the SS *Mont-Blanc*, a French freighter fully loaded with explosives, collided with the *Imo*, an unloaded Norwegian ship in a congested section of Halifax Harbor known as the Narrows. At this point, traffic was permitted to move in both directions simultaneously. Through a succession of avoidable mishaps that began with the *Imo* in the wrong lane, the vessel's excessive speed and the ineffective means taken by its crew to avoid running into the *Mont-Blanc*, the ships collided at 8:45 a.m. The *Imo* attempted to disengage by reversing engines, which caused sparks to flare inside the *Mont-Blanc*'s hull. The sparks started an uncontrollable fire aboard this ship laden with picric acid, benzol, TNT and guncotton. The *Mont-Blanc*'s captain, who quickly realized the inevitable blowup, ordered the ship abandoned. The crew, as it fled in lifeboats, shouted in an attempt to warn the oncoming rescue ships, but the shouts were unheard in the din of the roaring blaze. The fire attracted curious crowds on shore and in nearby buildings as the doomed ship drifted toward Halifax's Pier 6 and Richmond neighborhood.

An explosion with unprecedented force at 9:04 a.m. rained devastation of unimaginable proportions on Halifax and Dartmouth across the harbor. Over 1,500 were killed instantly, part of a toll that exceeded 1,900. Around 9,000 were injured, including hundreds who were blinded by shattered glass as they watched from their homes. In the aftermath, Halifax became a center for the treatment of eye injuries and remains so today. Over twelve thousand buildings in a sixteen-mile radius were destroyed or heavily damaged. Additional fires were started by stoves and lamps overturned by the force of the blast. These blazes consumed entire city blocks, trapped some victims in their homes and killed many more. An enormous quantity of water was vaporized and briefly exposed part of the harbor floor. A resultant tsunami sent waves as high as sixty feet above the Halifax shore's high-water mark and then swept shorefront victims into the water to drown. Halifax was the largest man-made explosion to date and remained so until the first test of an atom bomb. It retains the dubious record of the greatest loss from an accidental explosion. After Halifax, the United States Coast Guard, only recently assigned harbor security responsibility, installed explosives handling restrictions for New York Harbor, constraints that would impact operations at a number of facilities, including Gillespie.

Returning to Morgan, housing became scarce as hoards of newcomers associated with construction descended on the area. They fit where they could and took every available room in South Amboy. The entire third floor of the New Packer House (hotel) in Perth Amboy was taken over as quarters for construction supervisors. The usual desire to separate munitions operations from a residential population did not deter local real estate developer Charles L. Steuerwald, who found proximity to the new plant propitious to promote his new Bay View Manor development. Steuerwald, a native of South Amboy born in 1879, spent his early years in a varied

After initially serving as a residence for construction supervisors, the New Packer House in Perth Amboy became a headquarters for the press and a refuge for the displaced. It, too, became the scene of tragedy when on March 17, 1969, five were killed in a fire there.

business career prior to opening a Perth Amboy real estate and insurance office in 1914. The first section of Bay View Manor, located just below the South Amboy border, quickly sold out early in 1918, so he promptly readied subsequent sections for sale. Eager buyers may not have fully recognized the hazards of an adjacent munitions plant. While Steuerwald may not have been cognizant of the risks, he and his wife, Ethel, shared them. They lived in the historic former Conover estate, earlier known as Bay View Manor, which became the patronymic for his surrounding real estate venture. Theirs was the finest domicile in the region. Lot sales were initially vigorous at Bay View Manor, but despite this success, this section of Morgan was not built up until after World War II. While at the start of development Steuerwald was enthusiastic about this project and no doubt considered Bay View Manor a resume builder, he omitted any mention in his 1920 biography in Wall's *History of Middlesex County, 1664–1920* (volume 2).

The assembly of large workforces itself was a major challenge. The new loading plants and the enormous expansion of explosives raw materials capabilities would both fall short if the new workers did not meet quantitative and qualitative challenges. The military had already siphoned great numbers of younger, able men of the type from which factories ordinarily recruit. Other manufacturers, in growth mode to meet the war effort, competed for workers. However, two untapped labor resources became available. One was accessed by all shell-loading plants, while the other was specific to immigration centers such as the Sayreville-Amboys area. Locally, many immigrants who traditionally flocked to work in the region's various factories entered the munitions plants. Some did not speak English, but the lack of language fluency was no impediment for the performance of a repetitive task that depended on adhering to strict standards rather than skill. Good wages, although discriminatory, were an incentive. As the *Times* reported two days after the explosion:

> *The pay was liberal. Illiterate Polacks [sic], Russians, Italians, and others, many of whom could not speak a word of English, were making $8 or $10 a day. They received 47½ cents an hour, but when a man had loaded 250 shells he was credited with a day's work and was paid a cent a shell for each additional one. The girls got 37½ cents an hour, with the same privilege of earning extra money. Besides this they received time and a half for overtime.*

WOMEN AT WORK

The British head start with high-volume shell loading provided empirical evidence regarding the merits of women in loading plants. Many were hired there and not only performed admirably but also became essential to the war effort as Britain's massive mobilization and staggering battlefield losses created a major manpower shortage. Following Britain's experience, in the United States the growing armed forces would remove an increasing number of men from the labor pool. *The Iron Age* editorialized on women in manufacturing fields in its March 14, 1918 number, indicating that in this country women were first employed for lighter forms of work to fill manpower shortages in specific markets. Early assignments included

> *fuse work and similar operations which can be performed on drill presses, screw machines and other similar tools…Fuse makers in particular report that women have more patience with such small separations as drill press work, which becomes deadly monotonous to men workers…A Baltimore manufacturer believes it to be patriotic policy to employ women on work*

which they can do as well as men, so that more men may be released for the shipyards and other heavier forms of labor where women cannot so satisfactorily be used.

Indeed, while "Rosie the Riveter" is both well known and an esteemed fixture in our World War II homefront lore, "Shelley the Shell Loader," her industrial antecedent from the Great War, is virtually forgotten. In Great Britain, female war workers were employed on night shifts and appear to have held a wider variety of jobs. They poured molten lead for shot, operated lathes and built wooden boxes that carried loaded shells. The number of British women employed at war work greatly exceeded their American counterparts. However, the female force in America would have experienced even wider opportunities by necessity if the war had endured into 1919 as a result of the massive American offensive that was on the drawing boards at the time of the armistice.

Female war workers were given high marks for personal courage, an attribute that was motivated by the knowledge that loved ones were in combat. The aforementioned *Times* reported:

Fear of explosion is not shared by the women who were employed in the loading plants, numbering in all about 1,000. (This is believed to be a local figure.) These women held a meeting in Perth Amboy in the afternoon and unanimously voted to return to work in the plant as soon as the call comes for them. "Most of us have boys over there," said one of the women, "and we are all very anxious to do our part to aid in bringing the war to a speedy close. All of us know the danger to which we are almost constantly exposed, but it is nothing in comparison with that of our boys at the front. We want them to known there will be no delay as far as we are concerned."

Feminists strove to make the point that women could do whatever men could. Florence Bayard Hilles deserves special mention because this well-off, prominent feminist risked her personal safety to demonstrate her convictions about the ability of women to contribute to the war effort and their right for equal treatment in American life, especially regarding the vote. Hilles was the daughter of Ambassador Thomas F. Bayard and the wife of prominent Delaware attorney William S. Hilles. Her war activities had roots in Hilles's 1917 jailing for participation in a Washington suffrage demonstration. She took a job at a Bethlehem Steel shell-loading plant in New Castle, Delaware, which brought her notoriety as the "socialite munitions worker." While the length of her tenure in the plant is not known, a May 6 news item indicated that she had worked a week without incident. Hilles's purpose was to demonstrate her belief that the "only difference between men and women is a biological one. Where labor and law are concerned, they should be treated exactly alike." Hilles enjoyed a long career as a leader in feminist causes and was a successful sportswoman, having garnered numerous golf and tennis titles. She died in 1954 at age eighty-eight, according to her *New York Times* obituary on June 12, 1954. Rebecca West, the prominent writer who at the time was working for the British government, forcefully asserted the performance of women, taking note that they affirmed the capabilities expected of them, which prior to the war had not been put to the test. Her remarks, written for the *New Republic* and quoted in the *South Amboy Citizen* of February 16, 1918, included, "We are quite sure now. Women are good timekeepers; they can endure long hours; they can do work that requires delicacy of eye and hand; they are careless of danger; they are in every respect save that of muscular strength as useful as men."

After the war, the government was expansive in extolling women's efforts, noting that they made up one-third of all factory operatives of the New York District and stayed on the job with a much lower turnover rate. Girl recruits from "country districts" in New Jersey were singled out for their loyalty. Total turnover had been such a problem that although one firm hired 20,000 during its period of operation, it never employed more than 5,300 at any given time. The increasing difficulty of finding qualified applicants resulted in a regular lowering of qualification standards. Overall, women made up a majority of the inspectors in the district.

> *At the loading plants it was found that the following operations could be efficiently performed by female labor: Unpacking shell bodies, insertion of boosters, sealing of boosters, weighing (inspection), tending conveyor lines, loading propelling charge, weighing propelling charge (checking), painting rounds, stenciling rounds, inserting plugs, packing shell in containers, sealing boxes, moving containers, keeping stock and operating records. The opinion of the loading section was that "most of the operations of loading 75mm shell were carried out more efficiently be female labor than by male labor."*[18]

Since Gillespie did not reach its major production capability until summer waned, the plant could draw from the hoards of seasonal workers that staffed shore resorts. The income potential also attracted others who left prior positions. The Gillespie recruiter was said to have become a well-known figure in Asbury Park.

A sampling of munitions workers' backgrounds is gleaned from brief personal mentions in the press. Henry Byrnes of Red Bank had been that town's milk inspector. Arthur Tilton of Shrewsbury, who gave up teaching to become a mail carrier, made a second switch to Gillespie. Albert E.E. Strassberger was the proprietor of Stokes Hall in Ocean Grove, but the Grove was a summer seasonal operation. Some brick workers probably went to Gillespie, since the building industry was in the doldrums during the latter part of 1917. This forced a number of brick companies to close, including one Sayre and Fisher plant.[19] John H. Walsh, a checker at Gillespie, was the proprietor of Walsh's Hotel in Sea Bright. After he became ill with influenza on October 2, pneumonia developed and caused his death two weeks later. David B. Smith arrived at Gillespie after working on construction at Fort Dix. Indicative of the turnover, he soon left for DuPont.

The employment of shore residents who did not require housing led to a different challenge for the Gillespie firm: the cost of transportation. Transporting war workers from the shore was feasible, but the commutation rates were considered prohibitive, the previously cited liberal pay rates apparently notwithstanding.

Therefore, the question of special rates for war workers was taken up with the United States Railroad Administration, and a rate of six-tenths of a cent per mile plus 5 cents was established, with a minimum guaranty of $3 per mile per train. On this basis the fare from Asbury Park to South Amboy would be 21 cents one way, or 42 cents for a round trip of about 54 miles. As this was considered more than the war workers could afford to pay, it was decided that the Housing Corporation would purchase tickets from the railroads at the established special rate and sell the same to war workers through the various manufacturing plants at a uniform price of 30 cents per round trip and absorb the difference charges by the railroads. To mitigate housing and transportation, construction started shortly before the armistice near Ernston for a town of semi-permanent houses and dormitories to accommodate about 4,700 in the surrounding district.

On July 18, 1918, a train for the Gillespie Loading Plant was put on from Bradley Beach to South Amboy. This train started with 82 passengers, and inside of a week was carrying between 300 and 400 employees. On July 29, 1918, a second train for the Gillespie Loading Plant was inaugurated from Asbury Park to the Gillespie Co.'s

connection near Ernston, stopping at Long Branch and Red Bank.
These two trains also served indirectly the California Loading Co. and
other smaller war plants. [20]

This is the background behind the "munitions workers' train" reference occasionally found in the press. One account pointed out that plant workers, as are all travelers, were subject to the ordinary hazards of transportation. On September 28, 1918, Eugene Miller of Long Branch, as he attempted to board the munitions workers train at South Amboy, lost his hold, fell between two cars and was run over and cut in two. Ella C. Lloyd was killed in an automobile accident on September 20, 1918, as she returned from a photographer's after taking a picture for identification purposes.

Gillespie and other nearby munitions plants are known to have employed African Americans, but their participation is little known. The first clue I found is the illustration of the "colored barracks" from the Evans plant. The second is a brief news reference after the explosion of a hasty exodus of colored men from the several area plants who were returning to the South, a perhaps not unusual reaction at a cataclysmic time for those lacking local family or social support. [21]

The largely unskilled labor forces at the shell-loading plants were guided by close oversight and held to strict standards of performance. A shell-loading school was part of the Morgan facility. Numerous government inspectors examined scrupulously every finished product. Arrivals and departures were held in close check. Employees were searched for matches, which was only one of the safeguards taken to increase security. They were required to change clothes on arriving at the plant to minimize carrying in dust and small foreign objects. Special munitions worker boots were made without metal to preclude sparks. To enhance their personal safety, workers were required to shower on leaving to reduce health hazards of chemical exposure. The dangers of handling explosives mandated constant vigilance and reinforcement. Readers of the October 6 *Times* were aware that

it is impressed on all men and women employed at the plant from the first
that they are doing work as important as if they were in the trenches and
that their danger is as great as that of soldiers. When a man takes a place
there he is required to sign a statement to the effect that he works at his
own risk. The Government undertakes in case a man is killed to ship the
body to any part of the United States and pay the funeral expenses. If a
man is maimed he is pensioned. But no allowance is made to his family

if he is killed and, of course, it is impossible for any man employed there to be insured. The employee is reminded at every turn of his danger. Every building is placarded with warnings. The buildings are nearly all made of wood run up at the greatest speed. When the plant was built there was nothing in mind except speed production of the shells needed by the army and everything was sacrificed to speed...Officers of American and different allied armies visited the plant nearly every day telling the workers that the fate of the war depended on them as much as upon soldiers and that no man could do more patriotic service than keep his production at the height of his capacity. These officers said there was little choice from the point of view of safety between working in the plant and serving on the battlefield.

Munitions workers faced an additional hazard, exposure to a newly discovered, little known, but deadly occupational disease: TNT poisoning. Known precautions at the outset of the American buildup were minimal, but economics reasoned that reducing the amounts of escaped TNT would both save the value of the material and lessen exposure to the disease.

5

OCTOBER 4, 1918

A NIGHT OF HELL

Loading Building 6-1-1 Explodes

The explosion at 7:40 p.m. on October 4 tore apart production building 6-1-1 and killed nearly everyone inside. The worst of the destruction was yet to come. Firefighters sprang into action immediately, but the area fell into darkness with the loss of its power plant. Recall the elementary principles of fire protection: building construction, the nature of their operations, contents, the availability of an adequate water supply and, for multi-structure risks, the distance that separates the buildings. Shortcomings attributed to each of these criteria would plague the unfolding tragedy, handicap the firemen and preclude efforts to control damage. The first firemen on the scene immediately experienced problems, which were recounted by Charles R. Stryker, a captain in the plant's fire company. Their hose connection at a hydrant produced only ten pounds of pressure, too little to direct a stream of water. When the pumping station later reported the ability to produce 140 pounds, it became evident that the first explosion had caused a break in the water mains.

Captain Harry J. Riley took out the chemical and hose tender and quickly arrived at the fire in two minutes, only to find the 6-1-1 building flat on the ground and ablaze. Seeing that work on 6-1-1 would be futile, they turned their efforts in an attempt to save 6-2-1. However, prior to their reaching

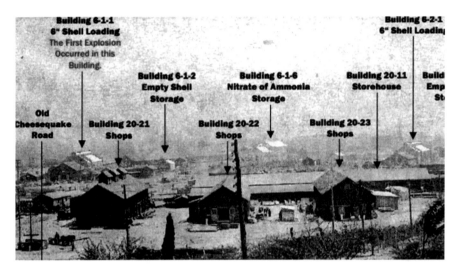

This extraordinary image depicts how the planned separation of structures in a shell-loading unit actually left them exposed to spreading fire. *National Archives. Annotation—Verne A. James Jr.*

it, an explosion of the magazine of 6-1-1 knocked each man about ten to fifteen feet, injuring a number of them, while Stryker held on to a telephone pole as wood and iron fell about him. Another explosion caused him to take cover behind a pile of railroad ties, where he observed the force of the blast carry a tie onto the road. A company from Rahway thought the pumper it brought might be effective, but the nearest hydrant was between 6-1-1 and 6-2-1—too dangerous a spot from which to operate. The Gillespie apparatus were then positioned just below the first aid office, where the men stayed until 2:00 a.m. Soon after they left to take a short break for coffee at the firehouse, an explosion rocked 6-3-1, which was followed by a second blast that blew in the end of the firehouse. Unable to reach their apparatus or 6-3-1, the men left the firehouse to protect themselves by taking refuge under the hill at Morgan station. They were told at 5:00 a.m. that it was no longer safe to stay there, so they moved on in the direction of Keyport. All lost valuables in the fire. Stryker added that 6-1-1 was known as the Jonah unit, as the building had blown down while in the course of construction and, in addition, several accidents had occurred there.[1]

An employee adjoining in building unit 9-2 gave this account, which was reported in the next day's *Asbury Park Evening Press*:

> *The first explosion was light, just a thud, but as it occurred the lights went out. Everyone thought that that meant danger and we all ran. I was hardly*

outside with about 20 other men when there was a terrific blast, which threw us all flat on the ground. We picked ourselves up and started to run, when another explosion bowled us over. The second one was in the part of the plant I had been working.

His recollection suggested that controlling the fire would be more than a minor challenge.

Government inspector Joseph Richard, who was in building 9-4, described the panic that followed the explosion, noting that the "men did not wait to take even their personal belongings but rushed out of the structures and made their escape. None of them was injured." Richard said more about the spreading alarm and the rush for doors as "workmen fled from all the other units and great bursts of flame shot high in the air, lighting up the yard. Out of this chaos, however, order was restored. The firefighting force of the plant started to work, while calls for assistance were flashed to all nearby points." Firemen quickly became aware of the perils of their work on hearing reports that twenty-five plant firefighters and guards were feared lost in the second blast. (Note that plant buildings, which were designated by three numerals, were at times referred to with two only. The numeric designations in the source references are retained here.)

When the lights dimmed, alarm spread, but this dimming appears not to have been caused by the destructive blast, which Roy Baxter recalled followed seconds later when the first explosions sent the men in his unit scrambling into the yard, where he saw that 6-1 had been "wiped out."

Baxter and his men ran into the swamp as they attempted to escape. He headed in the direction of his residence. As Baxter approached home, a shell tore a gaping hole through a wall, followed by a burst of flame. This close call motivated his change of direction, so he left in a hurry to go "across the reservation toward the administration buildings which front the main highway to New York, the eastern boundary." He was unaware of the fate of his companions as they struggled in the dark swamp. He recalled cries and explosions that punctured the night, "shells were now whistling through the air. It was a perfect hell. The explosion continually knocked us down. At the administration building we were told to get out as fast as we could. So, with several others, I started down the road and eventually arrived in Keyport." Baxter was not yet aware of the fate of his men but decided that Keyport was too close, so he headed south to Red Bank before continuing on to Asbury Park.

This scene of destruction is in the Ernston Road area. *Courtesy of John Ruszala.*

An unnamed employee in unit 9-2 described his reaction to the initial blast and then recounted the scramble to safety for the next day's *Times*:

> We kept on running for the open space between the collection of buildings and the high barbed wire fence which enclosed the whole plant. There was one great blast after another as we ran, accompanied by flashes of yellow light brighter than day, and as the big flashes disappeared the sky would be full of smaller explosions, as loaded and half-loaded shells, which were thrown into the air, exploded. Glass came down like rain, and pieces of steel from the shells and chunks of concrete would come down in a shower after each explosion.
>
> We were too busy getting away to stop to see what might happen to others, but it was plain that many of them, who were forced to run from the center of the zone of buildings to the outside, must have been killed as buildings blew up across their path of escape.
>
> When we got to the barbed wire fence we hunted for exits and could not find any. This fence is more than six feet high, built to keep out spies or curious people, but with one explosion coming after another, and danger that we would be hit at any minute, we all managed to climb over it.
>
> When we dropped on the other side we found ourselves in a swamp, which is another barrier to prevent outsiders from approaching the plant. The explosions were still going on, and we were about to plunge into the water when someone found some planks, and we got across on them to dry land. When I reached Morgan there were only 100 employees of the plant

there. Some escaped in other directions, but we all figured that the loss of life must have been heavy.

The place is wonderfully guarded and there is nothing in the theory that the explosion might have been caused by spies. Everyone is searched before he goes to work. No one is allowed to take in matches, and everyone is compelled to put on special clothes before he goes in, to make sure that he is wearing no metal buttons, which might strike something and cause a spark.

Each plant had a moat filled with water around it, to prevent fire from making its way along the ground from one building to another, and it was supposed that the buildings were far enough apart to keep an explosion in one place from blowing up another. As fast as the shells are loaded they are carried out to cars running alongside of each unit and taken away, so that there is never a large accumulation of shells. The T.N.T. is in melting machines in half loaded shells, in shells loaded and plugged with wood, and in magazines. These going off at different times caused the series of small and large explosions.

This man's report, which took the tone of a release from the Gillespie public relations office, appears to conflate his personal experiences with his hopeful belief in how the plant would operate and react to an accident. The hazards created by fire and exploding ordnance, along with the need to escape, precluded any one person's ability to give a blow-by-blow account of the unfolding destruction, but the initial reports indicated that units 6-3, 6-4 and 7-1, each located near the original explosion, were soon gone.

Fire companies from area towns rushed to Morgan, but their intentions were thwarted first by guards who were keeping all away from the danger zone and then from the collapse of the plant's water system.

Clergy were the only ones reported moving toward the fire. Chief O'Connell of the South Amboy police force reported seeing during the first night four young priests advancing in the direction of the fire. Later, when Middlesex assistant prosecutor John A. Coan, a resident of South Amboy, was asked to recount his personal experiences, he wrote an emotional "vivid pen picture," but he named three of them. One quotation suggests his dramatic flair, "Nor was the scene without its deeds of daring and bravery. Fathers Hayes, Quinn and Brennan went into the very mouth of the burning hell to sooth the wounded and comfort the dying." Another priest, Father Joseph Miller, was reported injured by a shell as he administered the sacrament of the anointing of the sick or last rites, as it was referred to at the time.

Many workers quickly disappeared in order to save themselves, but other persons rushed to the scene in seemingly hopeless attempts to mitigate unfolding disaster. The coast guardsmen who hurried into the danger displayed exceptional heroism. They had an early alert to the drama as Masters Mate K.S. McCann, on watch at Perth Amboy, was standing at a window when he saw the sky light up, so he called the cutter *Patrol* for an idea of the location, which the ship's keeper, Lester D. Seymour, told him was in the direction of Cheesequake Creek. Fearing for the safety of the barges at Gillespie where there were Coast Guard watchmen, Seymour promptly sounded the assembly signal to muster their seventy-five men when the first explosion burst. He then commandeered four civilian cars to shuttle his men to the plant and called the commander of the New York Division, Captain Godfrey L. Carden, who ordered First Lieutenant Joseph E. Sitka to take command of the Coast Guard response. Sitka took thirty men from the New York barge office with the ninety-four-foot harbor cutter *Calumet*, arriving at 1:30 a.m. on Saturday, while Carden ordered Lieutenant Frederick J. Birkett from Staten Island to Perth Amboy to help. Sandy Hook sent Cadet R.T. McElligott and thirty-five men with the cutter *Richard Caswell*, which would make a total force of about two hundred men. Larzelere's account claimed they arrived before any authority and found no one in charge, a void the Coast Guard filled by guarding the plant, bringing out the wounded, assisting with home evacuations and helping hospitals hold off hoards of anxious family members.

Gunner Charles S. Wright and Signal Quartermaster A.V. Horton took the cutter *Bluffer* up Cheesequake Creek in an attempt to tow away the loaded barges.[2] Extraordinary courage was shown by Ordinary Seaman J. Grimes, who, assisted by two soldiers, straightened damaged rail and then, acting as engineer, led out of the danger zone a trainload of TNT under conditions when smoldering fire threatened their immediate demise. Larzelere gave a similar account of Wright and Horton, who left their ship on foot, having moved a train out of danger, while the *Herald* reported Sitka's daring action on the rails: "Entering the burning area they skillfully maneuvered the dangerous trainload out of the danger zone and to a place of safety in a deep cut between two hills more than a mile from the flames. Near the spot where they removed the T.N.T. is a string of heavy coal cars some of them turned on their side and throw far from the rails by the explosion; all of them were scorched." Ordinary Seaman Clifford H. Bennett drove a car throughout the night into and out of the danger zone on a mission to carry out the wounded and bring in guards. He escaped death as his vehicle was repeatedly hit and had its door blown off. Keeper J.G. Hearon's experience underscored their collective risk and the chance of fate. After securing the Cheesequake gate, as he talked to a plant employee, an errant shell decapitated the latter. Hearon was unharmed. William S. Bennett secured the west gate in a section where artillery shells were regularly bursting. Robert Buchanan, a machinist in 6-1-1, claimed to have survived by having been blown through its collapsing walls. He told a reporter:

> *Suddenly, from a point a few yards away from me, there came a blinding flash. The floor seemed to rise beneath me. As consciousness left me I was conscious of a deafening crash and a deep red glow that seemed everywhere. When I regained my senses I was laying* [sic] *on the top of a box car which had been standing near building 6-1-1. The tremendous force of the explosion had simply lifted me from my feet, then rocketed me bodily through the air, out of the building and on the roof of the car. I knew that the treacherous bed I occupied was filled with explosive shells, likely to begin popping any instant. I was too stunned to rise to my feet, so I simply rolled from the roof of the car into what chanced to be a muddy ditch. Later I found myself stumbling up the Cheesequake Creek, which runs through the grounds occupied by the plant. I do not know how long I wandered about, dazed. Sometime after two o'clock another great explosion knocked me off my feet. I rose and stumbled forward again, half crazed by my hurts and by the ever-recurring explosions that came from behind. I was finally picked up by an ambulance and taken to Keyport.*

The Coast Guard response was heroic, as well as prompt; several men were decorated or honored for courage.

This scene of destruction is northwest of Ernston Road in the area of later streets including Gillen, Rota, Elaqua, Dielek and Driftwood Drives. *Courtesy of John Ruszala.*

Walker Hoffman saved lives by avoiding the natural instinct to let go of his burden at the time of the explosion. After remarking to a co-worker about the short wait for their meal break, he saw a big splash from 6-1-1 as the lights went out. But in recounting the event, the twenty-three-year-old Hoffman credited his foreman with heroism:

It was pitch black again and I had a loaded shell in my hands. My first impulse was to drop it when a big explosion threw us on our backs. But I held on. My left eye and the side of my head were in pain and then I began to hurt all over. I groped for a table and set the shell down. Maurice Annotee, foreman of our shed, came in with a searchlight. "Are you all O.K. and keeping your heads?" he yelled. "All here," we shouted. "On your stomachs and heads low," he commanded. We did so as requested just as more explosions not so big as the first one came. "I'll lead the way," he continued. "Follow me." Several of us had not been working at the plant more than a few days and we didn't know where to go in a case like this. The foreman surely had a cool head and saved our lives. We got to the door of our long, narrow shed and saw a big flare. The foreman shouted and we heard shells whizzing over us and breaking right and left. Then we got up and raced after the foreman to the barbed wire fence at the edge of the shed enclosure. I thought they might be charged with electricity, but I preferred death that way to the fire and explosives. We tore our clothing nearly off our backs scaling this wire. Then we hit one of the main roads. I don't know which one, my eye was hurting so.

Hoffman and a companion were picked up by an automobile and taken to a doctor for removal of shell fragments from his eye. They observed the pitiful state of refugees along the road, some with objects in hand that reflected their quick departure. Some still carried bread from their dinners, while one man held a tall lamp and another carried a parrot in a cage.

One could leave without knowing where he would be safe. Freehold men John Horn, a carpenter, and Samuel Hankins went to their rooms later in the night but were later routed through glass crashing from an explosion. The latter, a veteran of two wars, said the night seemed like a real battle to him. Joseph Wyckoff from the shipping department drove to work in his car that Friday. He escaped from the thick of the disaster but could not locate his vehicle a week later. The souvenir gathering began early. Joseph Koskey claimed that he picked up an eight-inch shell outside Ye Old Spye Inn on the day after the blast, apparently in the midst of the unfolding disaster, which he had placed in the window of the Freehold Trust Company. Their accounts were reported by the *Freehold Transcript* on October 11, 1918. The hazards of returning to one's room were reinforced by the construction crews, who were sent to repair the forty bunkhouses for the laborers that were located in the northeast corner of the 2,900-acre plot the flames had spared and which were only slightly damaged by the explosions. Some, however, had holes right through them where nine-inch shells had penetrated, according to the *New York Herald* of October 8.

Some simply stayed put. A young female telephone operator remained at her switchboard in the plant offices even after the first explosions smashed every window in the building while debris rained on the roof. The aged tender of the Morgan rail drawbridge stayed at his post from the first explosion until 10:00 a.m. Saturday morning. While his young assistant fled in terror, the old man remained there as shells poured about him. Several pierced the bridge, which remained in place. When evacuated, he was nearly deaf and was barely able to recount his experience.

Others watched in twisted awe. On Saturday, a *Sun* reporter found an expansive Mrs. Charles Seguine waiting on refugees who were crowded into the Y shelter while her husband was out on duty with the state militia:

> *Friday night was a night of hell…our home is on the bluff. I had a clear view of the flames. Horrible as it was, there was a dreadful beauty in it. Every kind of explosive made a different color—the T.N.T. made a color I can't describe. It was unearthly, but wonderful. There would be a burst of flame, a sword of flame darting up into the heavens, and then—I timed it with my watch—exactly fifteen seconds after would come the concussion. And when it came you fell to the ground; it seemed as if you couldn't live. The walls of my house which are wood, bent six inches from the perpendicular and then came back. It seems impossible, but they did.*

One wonders about reportorial embellishment throughout these accounts, suspecting that the woman in quotes would have braced herself after subsequent flashes. Her reaction may have been singular and not what Carrie Buckalew felt, as she told a reporter seventy years later, "The flares of the bombs as they were going off scared me. I was glad to get out of South Amboy."

Still others could not move. The aged and infirm who were unable to leave on their own faced the risk of abandonment if separated from family members, a not unexpected eventuality under the circumstances and a fate faced by Mrs. Mary Lawton, a nonagenarian who was half led and half carried by two young men into Red Cross headquarters. She was found in a wrecked South Amboy house from which it was thought everyone had left. No one knew where her mail carrier son was in the confusion. As the *Sun* reported, "The poor old woman sank into the chair they gave her, and—the pathos of it—lifted a trembling smile to the Red Cross girl that tended her. 'You're very kind, dearie,' she quavered." Or they were hurt prior to the awareness of danger. The 2:10 a.m. blast damaged Anna Rebecca Quin's home located nine miles away; falling plaster injured her head while she was in bed. William Hartmann, the bartender at Ye Old Spye Inn, was surrounded by falling plaster, but he chose to remain in dangerous proximity to the unfolding disaster. He may have questioned his decision judging from

The bartender of the Ye Olde Spye Inn stayed there throughout the explosions and fire. He braved staying in a locale close to the original blast where the loud reports of repeated explosions led him to believe that all might have been lost.

his comments to a *Newark Evening News* reporter (October 7): "The blow-up was so damned big I thought the whole plant had gone up and that it was all over, so we all turned over to get some more rest. It couldn't be done though because the plaster started to fall."

A small number were clueless, begging the "Red Cross to care for their children so they could go back to work the next morning. Sure the plant'll be working in the morning," they claimed with confidence. Even Thomas A. Gillespie was in the dark. He attempted to operate out of Perth Amboy but admitted a handicap of having lost all of his building plans and pictures in the plant office. His photographer, Andrew Coleman of Red Bank, also lost all of his equipment.

The best unprecedented and unique view of the disaster was observed by airmail aviator Robert Shank, who flew over the scene at the height of the "bombardment of shells and debris," presumably Saturday. He left an airfield in Philadelphia at 1:20 p.m. on a route to his Long Island destination that regularly passed over the Gillespie plant, which he used for a landmark without having given thought to its possible destruction. Mist was in the air and left him unaware of trouble ahead until ten miles from Perth Amboy, but then he saw that

Surviving Gillespie photographs are rare, which is understandable as plant photographer Andrew Coleman lost everything in the destruction. *Courtesy of Dorn's Classic Images.*

sticking up in front of me was a massive column of thick, greenish-colored smoke. I tipped my ship sideways and looked below. The roads between South River and South Amboy seemed as busy as Fifth Avenue. They were black with people. Hundreds of autos were racing along in both directions.

With a following wind I was making perhaps 120 miles an hour. In two or three minutes I was flowing over what the day before was the world's largest T.N.T. [sic] shell plant at an altitude of 4,000 feet. The place was unrecognizable.

The whole eight square miles [sic] that the plant covered was one vast volcanic crater of dull red flames, bursting shells and bright flashes as one magazine after another went sky high. Big cavernous holes told where a magazine or shop once stood.

Between me and the earth was a ragged bank of vile smoke....Not only was the earth below convulsed, but the very air was disturbed. My plane so rolled and rocked that it was all I could do to keep an even keel. Shells were bursting all around. It was like diving thru a barrage of archies [antiaircraft fire]...It looked as if some giant had dropped a bomb on an anthill.

Upon landing, Shank checked his plane for damage and was relieved to have found none. He vowed not to use munitions plants for landmarks in the future, claiming he would stick to "breweries, shirt factories and ladies' seminaries." It was claimed that this was the first time in history that a big catastrophe was described by a pilot who flew over it.[3]

A second view from the air was crucial in evaluating the spreading fire. Captain W.W. Watson of the Ordnance Department and Major H.L. Armstrong of the British army were observed making numerous passes over the fire in progress, repeatedly descending low over the flames to evaluate the prospect of their spreading. Upon reaching the ground, they conferred with local military officials over their findings. The group determined that the danger of fire spreading to the magazines was over, which enabled the authorities to permit a return to the evacuated areas. Contemporary accounts claimed that by hand they dropped bombs with careful precision on the edges of Cheesequake Creek in such a fashion that holes were torn in the banks that diverted water into a hollow and in turn flowed over the concrete coverings of some of the larger magazines—but admittedly without confirmation. While no later verification has been revealed, the bombing of the creek claim has become part of the explosion's lore. Similarly, it was reported by the *Sun* on the seventh that five barges loaded with explosives were sunk in the creek on the fifth because they could not be moved—another unconfirmed account.

Thomas A. Gillespie not only needed to ascertain the cause for future safety but also wished to allay the fears of a skittish public. He issued a statement late Monday afternoon, the seventh, which outlined the loss and attributed the cause of the explosion as worker error. Specifying the cause with depth, perception and analytical detail was a major accomplishment, especially when one considers its promptness. Gillespie's comments went on to address and explain recovery plans. His authority and insight merit an extensive quote from the *Newark Evening News* of the eighth:

> The T.A. Gillespie Loading Company plant consisted of 700 buildings of which 325 were destroyed. There were thirteen complete units for the loading of shells and twelve of these we know to have been destroyed. The thirteenth we have not yet been able to examine thoroughly, but it has been damaged. All of the cottages used and occupied by the superintendents and their families, together with the administration building, mess hall, etc., have been destroyed.
>
> The labor camp, consisting of forty buildings, is practically intact. The power house, docks, trackage system throughout the works, storage warehouses and magazines have not been damaged to any great extent.
>
> The first explosion occurred on Friday evening about 7:35 o'clock in 6-1-1 plant. From there it traveled to the 6-1-2 plant, and it is our opinion that that plant was destroyed by fire caused by the exploding shells from the first unit to go.
>
> In the 6-1-1 plant seventy-six men were working, twelve being United States Government inspectors. Of these seventy-six twelve are unaccounted for, including two inspectors, and the balance or a total of sixty-four, are missing, as less than this number of bodies have been recovered.
>
> Careful inspection of the site of the plant it is clear shows in all probability that the initial explosion did not occur either in the T.N.T. service magazine or in the low-pressure steam-jacketed amatol kettles as previously reported in the press dispatches.
>
> All of the available evidence points to the initial explosion having occurred in one of the regular operating rooms in which the 155-millimeter loaded shells were handled under established methods which have been successfully in vogue at this plant without accident for over three months. Any definite information as to the original cause is purely a matter of conjecture, one of the possibilities being an inadvertent act on the part of

one of the operatives, a risk of this character being unavoidable with an operation of this kind.

The spread of the fire and the subsequent events which involved the other units and part of the operating area of the plant were primarily due to exploding shells. The main storage area, including the principal magazines located at a suitable distance from the operating plant area, were not involved in any way.

It must be understood that this official report has of necessity been delayed, as incipient fires, following the principal explosions, introduced a risk which did not justify an inspection of the area until this morning, by which time the explosions had ceased and with the exception of a few small and isolated fires which are being extinguished, left the plant in a fairly satisfactory condition.

As regards the risk of any further fires or explosions, the work of cleaning up the area and reconstruction was commenced immediately following the careful inspection of the premises, the result of which is indicated in the foregoing. In controlling the situation from the outset the closest co-operation has been maintained with representatives of the Ordnance Department of the United States army, represented by Lieutenant Colonel W.C. Spruance Jr., assistant to the chief of ordnance. The property outside of the operating plant area is being efficiently guarded by the state militia.

Gillespie, the voice of knowledge and authority, spoke with confidence about his initial findings, but he was apparently wrong. Talk from surviving workers reached not only the press but also Middlesex prosecutor Joseph E. Stricker, who prepared a case for the grand jury. While Stricker was not talking, the accounts of employees reached the press, as early as a brief mention in the *New York Sun* on October 6, which also published Gillespie's theory two days later. The *Daily Home News* described in detail the overheated kettle account on October 14, 1918:

One of the employees in the plant, an expert in the chemistry of explosives, said that the amatol, in a kettle holding 1,500 pounds of the substance, became overheated and blazed up…

The workmen had prepared a number of shells for loading and proceeded to warm the amatol until it should have the proper consistency. In a short time it was seen that the compound was becoming overheated. Arriving at a certain point, amatol generates its own heat, and being aware of this, the men promptly shut off the steam and made efforts to reduce the temperature.

They worked at this for half an hour. There was a hose near, and if it had been used the catastrophe would have been averted. But this would have destroyed the amatol completely and the workmen sought to avoid this. In this they made their fatal mistake.

Suddenly one of the workmen saw that the amatol had reached the danger point and was about to flare up. He shouted a warning and rushed for the nearest exit. His watchfulness undoubtedly saved many lives. He had just passed through the door when the first explosion threw him forward headlong. Other men escaped the building only to be caught while fleeing through the plant.

Gillespie must have had access to those employees prior to making his statement, prompting one to wonder if his mistaken conclusion was deliberate in order to avoid legal or other liability. He was operating under a cost-plus contract, so the value of lost material probably was not of consequence to his firm. Adequate training and employees' adherence to proper work procedures were challenges to munitions plants, notably hastily organized plants with largely inexperienced staff. His initial avoidance of the cause of the accident and the motivation of the employees may never be known. However, this is not an implied indictment of the firm, its operation or employees. The experience of the army during the war led to the realization that the shell production of the hastily built industry shipped an inordinately high percentage of inadequate rounds that were also not sufficiently stable for long-term storage.

After the dust settled, the unfolding disaster was examined carefully by the army at an unspecified date. Their investigation was able to reconstruct events as they likely occurred with greater detail than Gillespie's analysis. While their report contains some conjecture, the account is amazingly clear, remarkably so when one considers that the extensive destruction eliminated so much evidence. The army noted that the initial explosion came without warning, an indication that the blast was not preceded by fire. Most survivors of unit 6-1 were unaware of what had occurred until they saw the wreckage. In addition, the fog of confusion, the fear of fire and the terror that anticipated the next big blast meant that the initial accounts would be personal but not thorough. Thus, the tone, in addition to the facts, vary in places from the newspapers.

Gillespie officers and employees who soon arrived at 6-1 found the central part, or kettle room, and the north end of the loading room wrecked and burning fiercely. Their testimony enabled the determination that the first explosion occurred in the loading section, likely in an amatol mixing kettle that contained 2,600 pounds of high explosive. A crater twenty-five feet wide and five feet deep suggested that "a second amatol kettle was thrown to the first floor by the first explosion and detonated from the burning wreckage exactly in the center of the building."

The first-arriving firemen were greeted by exploding shell in the shipping and painting rooms, together with popping boosters. The heavy explosion shortly after 8:00 p.m. was attributed to the detonation of between 200 and 475 shell stored in the shell hospital, which left a crater thirty-five feet wide and five feet deep. The narrative is continued with an extended quotation from Assheton:

> The first or second explosion set fire to the T.N.T. service magazine which burned to the ground, and also a car of T.N.T. on the side track just outside the service magazine was destroyed by fire.
>
> During this time, or from half to three-quarters of an hour, the firemen had been able to keep three streams of water on the burning unit. At about 8:25PM a third heavy explosion took place, which was probably the explosion of 800 loaded shell, which were in a car by the shipping room, and which made a crater four feet deep, thirty-five feet long, and 25 feet wide. This explosion caused the firemen and all others in the vicinity of the unit to seek temporary refuge from the bursting shell. About fifteen feet of the ten-inch water main was blown out by this explosion, and shortly after it was discovered that the water pressure was lost.
>
> Other explosions, probably consisting of small groups of shell in the painting and finishing room, formed craters on the site of the 6-1 unit.
>
> The exploding of boosters and individual shell or small batches of shell was continuous from 7:40PM to some time after what is called the third explosion, about 8:25 PM. Several persons, including two firemen, were injured by shell fragments during this period.
>
> After the third explosion, shell began to fly so fast that it was impossible for anyone to remain within the vicinity of the 6-1 unit, and all were forced to seek temporary refuge. All serious effort to check the spread of the fire and to protect the rest of the plant was abandoned, after breaking off the water line.
>
> Up until midnight, no serious destruction was caused outside of the 6-1 unit. An electrical warehouse and another small warehouse in which mails were kept had been set on fire either by falling shell or embers and had burned to the ground. Fire started in the 6-1 unit about 9PM and destroyed

the service magazine; but this fire died down and there seemed to be a reasonable expectation that it would not be communicated to the unit proper.

At or about 1AM, the fire in the 6-2 unit burst out again with great violence, and at about 2AM intense clouds of black smoke and brilliant flames issued from the unit, followed in a few minutes by a terrific detonation, probably due to the mass detonation of all the shell stored in the unit. This explosion formed a crater five feet deep, sixty feet wide and seventy feet long. Over this spot about 500 loaded 155 mm and eight inch shell had been stored.

It is probable that the detonation of these shell in the 6-2 unit threw hot shell on to the yard tracks and detonated a large number of carloads of loaded shell which were standing on a track near the unit. These carloads of shell exploded thereafter at reasonably regular intervals, and caused the detonation of three carloads of T.N.T. on the track between the 6-3 unit and the railroad yard. The detonation of these loaded cars completed the destruction of the water mains.

The detonation of the cars of shell may have projected hot shell into some of the storage buildings, and caused the detonation of other shell stored therein. The 6-3 and 9-1 units must have been practically demolished by the explosion of the three cars of T.N.T. on the main railroad track, and undoubtedly caught fire soon thereafter. Any attempt to state the order in which various buildings and units thereafter caught on fire or their contents detonated would be too conjectural to serve any real purpose.

A large crater was caused by the detonation of the contents of the 6-5 unit service magazine, containing 22,000 pounds of T.N.T. It made a hole fifteen feet deep and fifty feet in diameter.

The detonation of 38,000 pounds of T.N.T. in the 9-1 unit made a crater six feet deep and fifty feet in diameter.

Based on past experience, ammonium nitrate had not been in itself considered an explosive. The explosion at this plant proved, however, that when sufficient carbonaceous material is present with ammonium nitrate an explosive results which can be readily detonated. The probable explanation of these detonations of ammonium nitrate is that various ammonium nitrate storages first caught fire; that the ammonium nitrate was melted down by the heat of the fire, and that detonation resulted from the projection into this molten mass of one or more shell which detonated upon impact.

It seems probable that a heavy explosion which occurred about 4AM was either the ammonium nitrate storage in the 9-1 unit, containing 1,000,000 pounds, and which made a crater thirty feet deep, 140 feet

The World War I Middlesex Munitions Disaster

The explosion left about eight very large craters. The eruption at about 4:00 p.m. on Saturday of 1 million pounds of ammonium nitrate left a crater about 150 by 140 feet and 30 feet deep.

wide, and 150 feet long; or the ammonium nitrate storage in the 6-4 plant, which made a crater twelve feet deep, one hundred twenty-five feet wide and 200 feet long.

There were six craters made by the explosion of ammonium nitrate, but the size of the craters did not correspond with the quantities of ammonium nitrate stored in the magazines, which would indicate that in some cases only a portion of the ammonium nitrate detonated, the extent of the detonation presumably depending on the amount of carbonaceous material in the magazines, and the extent to which the flames had reduced the ammonium nitrate to a molten state before the projection of a shell into it.

The 7-1 unit was probably fired from loaded shell projected into it from the 6-3 unit, and the same cause started the fire which destroyed the 7-2 unit. The detonation of loaded shell in the 1-10 building was probably caused by a detonation of a mass of nitrate of ammonia stored in the 6-6 unit, from which fire was thrown to the 1-10 buildings.

Two smokeless powder warehouses were probably set on fire by the projection into them of shell which detonated on impact. The third smokeless powder warehouse was not affected by the fires in the other two, and remained intact.

Another interesting point in connection with the explosion was that large quantities of loaded shell, both in cars and in storage, detonated en masse, contrary to previous experience. The simultaneous detonation of more than 66,000 155mm shells, made a crater twenty-five feet deep, one hundred feet wide, and 600 feet long. Mass detonations must also have caused the large craters under eight cars containing 155mm shell.

All of the operating units within the plant were demolished, except the 4-1 unit which, though badly damaged by concussion, did not burn, and one or two buildings were still standing in the 7-2 unit. While the storage buildings themselves were more or less structurally wrecked, only five out of the forty-one were completely destroyed. None of the T.N.T. storage magazines located around the hill at the southwest corner of the plant burned or detonated.

The loss of materials was exacerbated by the presence of excessive quantities of volatiles. Over 30 million pounds of explosives were in magazines, storage and operating areas, as well as freight cars. Of this quantity, 12 million pounds were destroyed. Material was backed up in the Ernston rail yard because the plant's storage capacity was exhausted. Of the 1,013,453 loaded shell present on October 4, 308,239 were detonated or destroyed. Plant operations were geared to maximizing production in order to satisfy the heavy demands from the battlefields in France. However, shipping was bottlenecked due to a lack of lighters to remove completed shell. In addition, plant storage was strained by delays in the receipt of boosters for the loaded shells.[4]

The investigation considered other causes, notably sabotage. During the ensuing weeks, a variety of reports that included suspicious characters, smoking on the grounds, strangers speaking German or making anti-American remarks and the like were circulated and printed. No substantiation was found. Some present continued to voice unsubstantiated, even wild ideas, long into their lives.

Could the fire have been controlled? Fire prevention experts claimed they advised the company in June to install an automatic sprinkler system, which may have been of value in controlling the fire. However, one can understand their recommendation being ignored for a rushed project in a temporary building.

The preliminary *Report of Board Appointed by Ordnance Department Office Order No. 356 and No. 452 to Investigate and Report on the Explosion at the Plant* revealed that about eight very large craters and forty smaller craters were found, the sizable ones at points where loaded cars of TNT, loaded shell storehouses and ammonium nitrate storehouses were located. "One of the largest craters was located on the transfer railroad where three loaded cars of T.N.T. were known to have stood." The report suggested that the firm was not negligent and gave the executive and administrative personnel great credit for their accomplishments. It also cited each of the predictable shortcomings as enumerated elsewhere in this book. The most telling hazard cited is the congestion and inappropriate storage as a result of failure to receive needed shell components and inadequate transport.

A Population Leaves Home

The entire region, roused by the initial blast, was frightened into a high state of alert. Many in Morgan and its environs began to leave almost immediately. While Morgan was a sparsely populated locality, the city of South Amboy was devastated and suffered extensive property damage. Workers who made early escapes from the plant reported sightings of throngs already on the road, fleeing to uncertain destinations but just going away. The reports of the unfolding disaster became increasingly vivid as the blasts intensified. At 10:09 p.m., an ear-splitting crash "sounded as though the heavens had ripped open and were falling, pressing the air down in the descent." The earlier explosions had already set a frightened populace on edge, but this one appears to have prompted local officials to issue orders to evacuate South Amboy, which turned the early departures into a steady stream. Then, after the enormous burst at 2:10 a.m. on Saturday, the stream from South Amboy became a mass exodus.

The refugees traveled any way they could. The fortunate had cars, but any type of vehicle was pressed into service, especially trucks and vans. Trolleys would have been of greater utility, but the trolley wires adjoining the plant were blown down by the explosion, suspending service between South Amboy and Keyport. Those with family and friends in outlying regions fled to them. Others settled for whatever shelter, organization or place that could take them in. Or, as one stopped driver told a militiaman, "We're not going anywhere specially, we're just going away." Tent colonies sprouted up in Perth Amboy. Whole families were to be seen on the outskirts of Perth Amboy living in fields. "Small bonfires were burning

The care given to the injured included victims of shell shock. Alfred T. Kerr, the mayor of South Amboy, was hospitalized for this emotional harm. *Sayreville Historical Society.*

this morning and around these small groups and families were to be seen trying to keep warm."[5]

There were pathetic scenes on the streets of Perth Amboy: "Women were fainting in large numbers. As fast as they dropped they were picked up and rushed to the emergency hospitals for treatment. Children were to be seen running aimlessly about looking for their parents."[6] Those without wheels simply walked. Not knowing when they would return or be able to return, they carried what possessions they were able. Their bedraggled appearance made them appear as refugees fleeing a war zone, which indeed they were. The crowds were compared to Belgian refugees, the displaced people whose repeated images of abandoning devastated towns had made them symbols of an engulfed continent and had rent the hearts of a watching world. It was often repeated that martial law, the most extreme form to regulate a breakdown of control, was declared, but no official pronouncement has been found. The local press did not print stories critical of local behavior, but a hint was suggested by the testimony of Captain Oliver A. Phelps for the Third Deficiency Appropriation Bill, who told a United States Senate subcommittee on June 5, 1919, "Immediately following the explosion, you know, there was a sort of a reign of terror in that section."

Soldiers patrolled the streets to maintain order and prevent looting. Few incidents were reported. However, one government commentator suggested in postwar testimony that things were rather rough right after the explosion.

As houses shook, their residents feared collapse. However, most houses were spared major structural damage, but nearly all lost windows, and in addition, some chimneys were placed in precarious condition. Many who did not leave immediately camped outdoors all night in fear of falling buildings. Joseph Karcher, who would enjoy a long career as an attorney, writer and speaker, was a teenager at the time and recalled seeing people staying in the fields across from the family home at 500 Main Street, Sayreville. As the explosions continued into the night, accounts of their intervals varied. The discrepancies may have originated because several reporters were counting blasts of different intensity. One remarked that "at every major blast the trembling of the earth was heavy enough to throw people from their feet in South Amboy and Perth Amboy."[7]

The Steuerwalds did not fare well with their impressive domicile, Bay View Manor, the former Conover estate, which they had occupied only in June. The house was wrecked, but they escaped injury. Anna Morford related to me that Mrs. Steuerwald had told her that they had been out of town during the explosions but on their return found little more than standing chimneys. They had lost everything.

While the population was generally moving en masse away from the scene, other residents headed toward the plant. These were anxious family members of the many workers living in the immediate area who headed to the danger zone to inquire about their loved ones' safety. Gillespie guards,

Some frightened area residents spent the night in nearby fields, as they feared the collapse of their houses.

While there was some significant structural damage in South Amboy, it was, for the most part, limited. However, most glass was destroyed. *Courtesy of Sayreville Historical Society.*

A standing chimney underscores the extent of the devastation and how some owners had the misfortune of their buildings receiving the full force of the explosions.

their numbers having been boosted by soldiers stationed nearby, rushed to take control and quickly cordoned off the plant for security reasons. Their actions kept fearful relatives in the dark. One account observed that "about the entrance to the barbed wire enclosure was an excited crowd, some almost resisting the guard in eagerness to get news of relatives who had worked at the plant and had not returned to their homes. At intervals the crowd fell back as an ambulance came clanging through the gates and disappeared in the darkness." Another account in the *Daily Home News* of October 5 observed that "the wives of many men who lived near the plant approached the scene with utter disregard of danger and made wild efforts to pass the guards at the two gates that are placed at the two ends of the property. At times the guards were forced to handle the women roughly to prevent them from rushing into the danger zone, and the women clung feverishly about the groups of men who actually left the place unhurt to beg for some word concerning their own loved ones." In South Amboy, crying women and children filled the streets, begging to be told who had been killed and who had escaped. As the authorities expanded the security zone, reporters became victims of an effective news blackout.

The general direction was northward across the county bridge over the Raritan. Joe Rzepka recalled many years later how the bridge was wooden then

The Steuerwalds moved into Bay View Manor in June, but their stay there was brief. The former Conover estate, the most impressive house in Morgan, was left in ruins. *Courtesy of Sayreville Historical Society.*

Joe Rzepka recalled his thoughts during a nighttime escape to Perth Amboy over the small, narrow County Bridge, "If one of them shells hit that bridge, we were finished."

and filled with people. As they hurried across, he realized, "If one of them shells hit that bridge we were finished."[8] Maurice Steiner told Frank Yusko, who in the 1990s interviewed many residents who lived through the explosions and aftermath, "Every time there was a blast the bridge would shake."

Victoria Farley, who was on the bridge at Milltown, "didn't know which way to run." She added that many refugees came to Milltown and stayed for a couple of days, some having been given refuge by her father and others by the German Reformed Church. A then fifteen-year-old Florence Stolte stayed at the Rahway Prison, where she recalled the nice and polite prisoners who gave up their cots for their short-term visitors. Dorothy Kern was shaken up by the experience occasioned by her carrying her brother upstairs and then nearly dropping him from the shock of the blast.

Carrie Buckalew, then twelve, recalled seventy years later having been at a friend's house, which she fled. Electric wires fell down near her as she ran on a nearby street. Power was later cut off to avoid the potential for electrocution. Peg Uhrin, also twelve, recalled that as she emerged from a movie theater, she saw the sky light up. Her parents, who had earlier cautioned their children to be prepared to leave, realized their worst fears when "we were in bed and all the windows broke around us." They headed north, an experience she recalled for the October 4, 1988 *News Tribune*: "It was the most pathetic thing. People were crying and carrying their things in bags. We were just so happy to be alive." Sadie Tarallo Ruszala told me that while she was in a nearby butcher shop with a friend, the first blast went off, resulting in a frightful run home. The explosions were so forceful that they opened shut doors. The next morning, she was at her aunt and uncle's grocery store on South Pine Avenue when a strong blast blew groceries and jelly rolls into the street. They then fled to Newark by automobile.

Vice-president of the loading company, E.A. Yates, who had joined Gillespie four years earlier as an engineer, issued a warning on Saturday morning claiming that if the fire reached the TNT storage magazines, a blast of unprecedented force and widespread devastation would ensue. The more extreme estimates of the area of potential destruction do not merit repetition, but presumably no one knew for sure. After his pronouncement, the instinctive exodus became a forced evacuation of Morgan and South Amboy. Thomas A. Gillespie, who felt otherwise, issued a statement later attempting to allay public fears as he pointed out that the big magazines were well hidden in the earth.

Refugees stepped into Perth Amboy, which was by early Saturday morning described as a "windowless city though not so completely devastated." Then

The long lines of refugees who fled the area on foot were compared to Belgian war victims. The *Times* reported that this group was headed in the direction of Perth Amboy.

the 10:09 a.m. blast took out the remaining storefronts and prompted more to leave that city, too. Ramon Montalvo, a shop owner on Smith Street, experienced unusual difficulty. He boarded up his windows after the glass was blown out, but afterward the boards were similarly taken down. Pedestrians in Perth Amboy were forced into the street in fear of flying glass. The New Packer House assumed dual roles of a shelter for the wounded and as headquarters for reporters who were thwarted in their efforts to reach the scene. The Perth Amboy General Hospital overflowed. Some fled to the police station. Boardinghouses strained as they took in whatever numbers could be squeezed in their cot-lined places.

The stories of participants and survivor stories told decades later require a credulity test. Fading memories and a penchant to exaggerate or embellish mean the reliability of some accounts might range from hardly to not at all. Mike Nagle, who later became South Amboy's fire commissioner, told how he and some companions took on an unusual care-giving role. They liberated whiskey from liquor stores. Whiskey at times has been used as an emergency anesthetic and also at one time was believed, according to Nagle, to have had curative powers. He claimed they broke some liquor store windows to secure a whiskey stock for the local hospital. Did they? Most windows were

The World War I Middlesex Munitions Disaster

This scene of carrying away an injured victim is recognizable today in South Amboy as the southeast corner of South Pine and Bordentown Avenues.

Residents left by any means possible, including horse and wagon, or simply walked.

broken, cautious shopkeepers removed goods from their window displays and streets were heavily guarded. I simply ignored some accounts that failed the believability test.

Residents close to the plant on the south fled in the direction of Keyport. Some residents of that town and nearby Matawan did not feel safe there, so they joined the refugees in efforts to seek safety in the backcountry and places beyond. Help was forthcoming to those who stayed. Keyport mayor Bogardus took many of the homeless into his own residence. Others were admitted to the East Keyport schoolhouse and the Matawan Seed Company. The Crine Seed Company opened a building as a shelter.

Eighty orphan boys around five and six years old abandoned the New York Foundling Asylum at Huguenot, Staten Island, after spending the night in a panic-stricken state as the ground around them shook. They attracted considerable attention upon their arrival at the South Ferry Terminal in Lower Manhattan. The unusually well-behaved boys were led by three nuns who attributed their model obedience to fear. While their destination is unknown, New York armories were opened and furnished with cots.

AID ARRIVES

As residents fled, a massive relief campaign was organized through the American Red Cross and sent to the Amboys. Major assistance was also contributed by numerous local groups, which coordinated their efforts with the Red Cross. In addition, many community organizations provided aid by turning over their facilities to house and care for a displaced populace. The Boy Scouts were especially helpful in ways suitable to their youth. Their first need was to evacuate stragglers who avoided the early exodus that began after the enormous blasts in the middle of the night. They also needed to find shelter for many who set out on wayward paths in the dark without knowing where they were heading because they had no place to go. Armories, police stations, transportation terminals, railroad stations, schools, churches and clubhouses were among the facilities that took in the temporarily homeless. As was noted, relatively few houses suffered major structural damage, but South Amboy was also virtually a windowless city. The Red Cross was afforded headquarters at the Board of Trade Building and the lawn of St. Mary's School, the two locales in Perth Amboy and South Amboy, respectively. Most of the relief response information recounted herein is included in a report by Dr. Thomas J. Riley, a special representative, Department of Civilian Relief, American Red Cross. This statistics-laden tome, written with a deserved self-congratulatory tone, is cited in the bibliography. The report gives credit to the major assistance provided by the National League for Women's Service and the Motor Corps of America, groups that were of critical help, especially in moving people around and making section trips of the area.

Organization was the first challenge faced by the Red Cross upon their arrival on Saturday morning. One stroke of good fortune was finding that nearly all had been housed and fed for the night. In one example, over one thousand persons found respite under the roofs of four Perth Amboy shelters, which were aided by cots received from the New York Red Cross and the Raritan Arsenal hospital. As the Red Cross prepared for a service of an unknown and perhaps protracted duration, it began its initial operation handicapped by turned-off electrical power. In addition, its fieldwork required a massive glass replacement project and the need to ensure that in South Amboy each chimney was inspected for safety.

Overnight housing was far more challenging than accommodating overflow crowds at a seashore resort. In one instance, about eight hundred who walked to Sewaren in Woodbridge Township were offered an old, decrepit hotel that had been closed for five years. Sanitary conditions were poor, yet places on the floor for the masses and beds for the ill and injured were utilized to provide makeshift shelter. Three women forced an unusual health challenge; they gave birth en route. Two were sent to a hospital, while one remained at the "hotel." The flu became the real health crisis.

The Gillespie explosion was concurrent with the worldwide Spanish influenza pandemic, which would kill unknown tens of millions, with the lower estimates in the range of at least 50 million; others believe the toll may have exceeded 100 million. As they made their rounds, local caregivers discovered infection, which required a variety of responses and relief. At times, an individual was sick, but in other instances an entire family was infected. In one pitiful case, nine ill members of a family were gathered in one room. They were cared for by a fifteen-year-old daughter, run down by her own symptoms, who had been unsuccessful in obtaining a doctor. Young children were suddenly orphaned. In one sad instance, a four-month-old was found alone after first the child's father and then its mother died.

Temporary hospitals were established as the cases mounted, including one at Perth Amboy in St. Peter's Parish House, Rector Street, where thirty beds were provided. Later, the Elks Club was commandeered for a hospital. This compelled the Red Cross, which had its workroom there, to find other quarters. They soon relocated to the YMCA hall.

Some families became separated, having been parted as a consequence of confusion, illness or even language barriers. After one family of nine fled hurriedly by foot following one of the massive nighttime blasts, they were reportedly running in the mist when one daughter became separated. Her parents discovered her only after having been taken by automobile to Elizabeth. After another family arrived intact at the Elizabeth armory, their ill son was transferred upstairs for care but was later taken to a hospital. His father's lack of English made it extremely difficult to reunite with his son.

One could readily slip from public or private view during the confusion, so a report of a missing worker was not regarded as tantamount to an unidentified death. Helen G. Timko, a Red Cross volunteer, set up an information bureau to assist families. She had similar prior experience six years earlier as she sorted the names of those on the sunken *Titanic*. Timko's activities were reported by the *Times* on September 17, 1920, when she was engaged in similar work at another Morgan, the banking house on Wall Street that had been struck by a terrorist's bomb. Typical of the confusion was the missing plant worker who was taken to a hospital after suffering from a night of exposure. His family learned that he had survived only as he sought to contact them.

As the pandemic rose to a peak, some caseworkers either became ill themselves or had to return home to care for infected family. The available doctors became overwhelmed, but it was difficult to supplement their numbers as demands for their services were all over the region and the military had taken many of them. It was estimated by Monday night, October 7, that there were 5,000 cases of influenza and 250 cases of pneumonia just in Perth Amboy.

As the caregivers themselves needed quarters, the Perth Amboy Public Library rose to assist by its temporary conversion to a Hostess Home for Red Cross workers and Motor Corps women.

The Red Cross received numerous requests for housing assistance. While it regularly reevaluated its role, although mindful that its mission was essentially humanitarian relief rather than emergency home repair, the Red Cross realized that getting people back in their homes would reduce the demand for temporary care. After the issue was referred to its War Council, the Red Cross determined that it was able to motivate prompt action by local contractors and urge the Pittsburgh Plate Glass Company to speed glass replacement.

The Red Cross did provide small sums of cash assistance in some instances, but it found that most families had adequate funds. In addition, the munitions plants paid hefty wages, adequate local housing was available and the people were basically frugal.

After their valiant efforts to combat the influenza epidemic, which strained available medical resources, the Red Cross issued a sanguine evaluation of the disease's local impact, which merits quotation from the cited work:

> In the judgment of the medical director, the influenza at South Amboy was of a comparatively mild type. This, and the fact that the weather was most favorable, allowing of persons to remain in the open air the greater part of the day, and the fact that the houses were without glass in the windows, insuring good ventilation even in the case of overcrowding, and the early opening of the playgrounds, accounted for the rapidity with which the epidemic was checked and the very low mortality.
>
> The number of pneumonia cases was not excessive, considering the shock and exposure through which persons had passed, owing to the explosion at the Gillespie Plant and the great discomfort, due to the lack of cooking and heating facilities in the homes. The mortality, taking all things into consideration, was low, and this may be attributed to the careful personal attention given by doctors and nurses to each case; the very excellent quality of the drugs, and especially to the fact that the majority of cases were kept in the open air day and night.

The canteens were closed on Sunday, October 13, and after an additional week, the medical social service department was also ended as the Red Cross then contributed to a South Amboy community program.

Riley's report followed some months later when he could include a financial accounting and his recommendations for organization after disasters. Riley, who was a recovery specialist, did not linger long in the area as he left for Brooklyn to supervise relief after the November 1, 1918 Malbone Street subway wreck that killed nearly one hundred people.

The most helpless of creatures were left behind. Residents were separated from pets, but also at the time many kept horses and farm animals. Plant workers were immediately aware of the fright of the former. Timekeeper Murray Rosenbaum, who was working adjacent to 6-1-1, told the *Sun* on

October 6, "It was a fearful thing to see the horses of the construction men dashing away, driverless, wagons behind them, the poor things mad with fright, bound for heavens knows where."

Some residents who had fled sought to return home prior to official clearance, insistent that they be able to care for unfed horses and chickens, as well as cows that had not been milked. Enabling evacuees to leave with their pets remains an emergency preparation challenge for reasons hardly needing explanation. One heartfelt scene was witnessed at the Perth Amboy YMCA, where a little woman in black, the wife a plant worker residing less than half a mile from Gillespie's, who on arriving described how their home's contents were blown around them. She brought her small son, who "led a tiny, trembling mongrel...but they saved their dog and the small boy hugged it fondly, giving it bites of the sandwich a kind YWCA woman have him."

The number of explosion/fire deaths specified in initial reports was exaggerated. Actually, a true figure will never be known. Two figures more often cited than others are sixty-four and ninety-four. However, one can presume that the actual number is higher. Gillespie himself calculated the lower figure by projecting the number of workers in 6-1-1 at the time of the explosion, which he then reduced by the number that was later accounted for. This poor methodology would not account for casualties elsewhere at the plant. In addition, he may not have known with certainty how many were in that building, as personnel records were destroyed, an unfortunate loss that complicated matters. The higher number was projected by Dr. John W. Trask, medical director of the United States Employee's Compensation Commission in Washington. His title suggests that his calculations were focused on the workers' compensation claims filed on behalf of the deceased. This methodology would not have included other deaths. The *Times* reported on the sixth an injury figure of 150, excluding minor hurts, and projected that "many of the injured will die," not unlikely as the treatment of burn wounds at the time was nowhere near as effective as it would be by century's end. Another observer who was quoted in anonymity expected a much higher toll, as he claimed, "Most of those killed were blown to pieces while running from the center of a maze of building, freight cars and motor trucks blowing-up and wiping them out, scores at a time."

With respect to the disaster having coincided with the worldwide influenza pandemic, popular belief claims that local flu casualties were exacerbated by post-explosion conditions, which helped spread the disease among a populace weakened by its evacuation treks over long distances and congregating in crowded shelters. Close contact with the infected propelled the spread of the disease. However, this claim is contrary to the aforementioned contention of the Red Cross that influenza mortality here was lower. The possible impact of the pandemic could be best demonstrated by the comparison of influenza mortality in the Sayreville/Old Bridge/Amboys region with influenza deaths in comparable areas of New Jersey. Referring again to the explosion, early reports estimated the number of bodies carried out, although many in the first groups were not identified. Medical forensics was not advanced in a manner that can establish identification from a small fragment of flesh or bone. Trask later became the medical director of the United States Marine Hospital, Port of Boston, and an assistant surgeon general of the United States.

Why and how did some die? Chance and varied circumstances accounted for a number of the unexpected appointments with death. Roy E. Hickerson was rejected for army service and was able to have continued as an officer in his father's Brooklyn furniture business. However, he was determined to help the war effort. He wrote home on his fatal first day at Gillespie that he had begun work as a government inspector. He was identifiable by only a ring given to him by his mother. Eyewitnesses claimed that some who were attempting to flee in the surrounding fields were killed there, but their reliability is questionable. Thomas Gash of Red Bank was believed to have suffered such a fate, but he was unaccounted for over a month's time. Eventually, his body was found in the ruins near an apparently collapsed creek bank. Weeks also passed before the body of John Parker was located in the ruins where he was last reported seen. He was identified solely by body fragments that reflected "peculiarities of the skull and jaw." A card carried by Henry Byrnes of Old Bridge was his only means of identification. Many injured were rushed to hospitals; some died there. Guard Charles H. Morris of Long Branch lingered unconscious at Perth Amboy for ten days. His family was not aware of his location until two of his daughters found him just before he passed away.

A plant hospital, erected outside the plant grounds, was nearly complete at the time of the explosion. While initial reports indicated that it was not operational, on the eighth the *Times* described the first efforts to use the facility:

> *Early in the evening of Friday the first rescue work was done in the Gillespie Hospital at the works. The service rendered there had all the thrills and dangers of field hospital work under fire at the front. Shells were bursting, tongues of flame flared every few minutes and the groans of the wounded*

filled the air. To add to the horror the electric lights gave out four times and left the relief workers and their patients in the darkness. Again and again as the building would rock upon its foundations, the nurses were urged to leave the place, but they stayed at their posts until the terrific explosion of 11P.M. Then, when the structure was evidently doomed, they brought out their patients and repaired to South Amboy.

Presumably, they continued elsewhere as South Amboy facilities were not only inadequate but also destroyed. Some were taken to the new United States Army Base Hospital in Colonia, Woodbridge Township, which was opened earlier in the year to treat wounded returned from France.

Early usage of the term "hospital" could be applied to a variety of care facilities that housed multiple patients. South Amboy was served by a "City Hospital," not unlike the first hospital in many small towns, a place with few beds that was installed in a former residence. It did not survive the blast, as the *Daily Home News* reported the next day, "The South Amboy Hospital was badly destroyed [*sic*] by the concussion of the explosion. The first of the wounded taken from the plant were rushed to this hospital for treatment. They were cared for until six o'clock this morning when part of the roof of the building was blown off and every window in the institution broken." The South Amboy Memorial Hospital was formally organized after the recovery. A substantial donation from Thomas A. Gillespie helped its establishment. The hospital was opened in 1924, greatly expanded about fifty years later and remains in place between Bordentown Avenue and Highway 35.

The attribution of death by disease as a consequence to exposure at Gillespie was, as noted, speculative. In addition, the ability to establish the cause of death was not the advanced science it would become decades later. However, the families of victims by other causes did not need to be convinced of the impact the explosion had on their losses. After Florence Heyer of Perth Amboy died October 17 at age twenty-three, her passing was attributed to shell shock from the explosion. Elvira P. Barr, age unknown, a stenographer at the nearby DuPont plant, died on November 5 from "nervous shock." The government paid serious attention to the emotional distress of some, notably the case of Mary Lynch, who, while alone, visiting at Morgan, was sent by the explosion wandering in a demented condition. Congress passed a bill to pay $10,000 on her behalf to her sister. Miss Lynch, then thirty-eight, was confined to a mental hospital in a state from which she was not expected to recover. James W. Griffith of Red Bank died in November 1918 from having stepped on a rusty nail.

Coast guardsman Herbert E. Ketchani was at South Amboy on October 4 when a section of his vessel's pilothouse and other parts of the boat were carried away in the blast. While Ketchani was ashore engaged in rescue attempts, he caught a severe cold. Pneumonia developed and caused his death at age twenty-three on November 4. John Brown Jr., an eighteen-year-old state militiaman, contracted his deadly pneumonia while doing guard duty. Gillespie employee Frank X. Herrman, age thirty-six, contracted his fatal pneumonia during rescue operations.

Elsewhere in the Region

The loud retorts reverberated across the Monmouth County border. Anna Morford, whose family, the Charles Hendricksons, operated the Cherry Tree Farm in Middletown, added that they heard the blasts and felt the ground shake. They saw a crowd of refugees who had left Keyport and were heading south. Some stopped for rest on their lawn and were given sandwiches and coffee by Mrs. Hendrickson. Her brother had contact with a state policeman who warned of the feared explosion of the storage magazines, which prompted the family to leave the county for a night at a shore hotel. The Hendricksons learned on their return that their church, Middetown Baptist, had suffered considerable damage to its windows.

In Middletown, egg and chicken farmer Robert Eigenrauch told me in 1993 that they opened all their windows as Gillespie blew to prevent glass breakage. The plant at Morgan became part of his farm. Bob was active at the surplus sale and was able to build much of his farm from lumber salvaged at the plant. He extolled the merits of their three- by six-inch spruce. Years later, the peaceful environs of his farm located on the road from the township's Fairview to Chapel Hill sections would be shattered by another great blast, this in peacetime. In 1958, the explosion of a NIKE antiaircraft missile located a short distance away killed ten and unsettled an area that had been assured when the missile battery was installed that such an accident "couldn't happen."

The explosion was heard at Camp Vail, a new communications facility in the Eatontown-Oceanport area of Monmouth County. This signal corps base was rattled by the blast, about which a soldier, identified only as "G.H." wrote home. He told his family on October 8 that he was well but quarantined due to an influenza breakout at the base, but also that "a big ammunition plant got blowed [*sic*] up." His tale blended alarm with courage: "It was about 16 miles away from our camp and kept us awake all that night. It was nothing but bang, bang all the time. It certainly did shake our barracks and rattle the windows, but did not scare me any." Camp Vail, which had sent 1,500 soldiers to guard Gillespie's, was renamed Fort Monmouth not long after it was established during the war. The base became one of the premier electronic warfare research and development facilities in the world. Until its recent closing, its museum exhibits included one of the war's communications heroes: a carrier pigeon. These birds proved their crucial value in the delivery of battlefield messages, a means that saved many lives.

Downtown New York had hardly recovered from the shattering it had received fourteen months earlier from nearby Black Tom. As the ground trembled from the distant Gillespie explosion, wary New Yorkers remembered how close the war could come. The Standard Oil Building at 26 Broadway, which shivered nervously after a big blast, was evacuated at noon the next day prior to the Saturday half-holiday. Selective other nearby buildings were also closed. After city hall doors were blown open by one of the heavier blasts, a patrolman suspected a bomb might have been placed there. Across the street, the Hall of Records lost eight stained-glass windows. Buildings as far north as above 100th Street were reported to have shaken.

Loss of glass was scattered over a wide area. The Gillespie New York office was located at Hudson Terminal, two massive structures on Church Street that were demolished for construction of the World Trade Center. They issued instructions from there to open windows to reduce the possibility of breakage. The Produce Exchange Building, located at 2 Broadway, a block from Standard Oil, but later razed, suffered extensive glass breakage, fifty windows on the Broadway façade. The Custom House across the street lost forty-five panes. However, the nearby Whitehall Building at 17 Battery Place reported only one broken pane. Some breakage was reported as far north as 50th Street. The southern sections of Brooklyn, which were not shielded by intervening structures, were hard hit, including Coney Island, Brighton Beach and Bay Ridge. Some glass loss was suffered at other Long Island towns.

New York anticipated and was braced for the worst possible scenario at Gillespie. Following the receipt of the aforementioned Yates warning on Saturday morning and with recollections of how the Black Tom blast was felt on the East River Bridges and the Hudson River rail tunnels, the authorities feared that an explosion of the main TNT storage magazines could significantly damage or impair them. As a precaution, city bridges and tunnels were closed to traffic until the danger of that potential catastrophe passed.

RECONSTRUCTION AND THE END OF WAR

On the morning after the explosion, the Allied forces remained heavily engaged in action on the western front and maintained their undiminished need for an expected massive supply of shells. Only in retrospect did the commanders realize that the war was in its active final stages. Not only was this not evident at the time, but also, the great progress being made by the Allies in October 1918 notwithstanding, the Allies were forming plans for even greater offensive actions for 1919. Thus, in order to minimize the potential for a reduction in the flow of shells to France, the government announced two-fold action. It would immediately undertake the reconstruction of Gillespie and would increase production at the other loading plants. The Ordnance Department was wary, however, that reaching the additional production to make up for the loss of Gillespie would strain the capabilities of the other plants. Gillespie claimed to have loaded 32,000 shells daily, or about 1,000,000 monthly. The stated claims for its expected eventual output ranged from 50,000 to 74,000 daily. The first challenge at Morgan was debris removal. The illustrations vividly portray not only the utter devastation but also a site that was literally littered with twisted and broken metal, splintered timber from shattered buildings and wrecked vehicles, equipment, material and sundry supplies.

Unexploded ordnance made the grounds tantamount to a domestic war zone. Gillespie immediately advertised a call for 1,500 men to clear the mess, while a crew of skilled craftsmen was assembled for the reconstruction that would start as soon as the ground was clear. The nearby California Loading and Oliver plants became wary of reports that they were down as a consequence of the explosion, so they published ads that asserted that they were not affected by the disaster. As these two plants soldiered on with continued operations, they faced the reality that worker fear following accidents nearly always reduced nearby munitions employment. However, one can presume their defections were short-term, as was often the case.

As was noted, Gillespie and the government undertook investigations immediately after the accident to determine the cause. The knowledge of causation was necessary not only to improve safety at other loading plants but also to quell the inevitable speculation that follows every tragedy. Rumors were running rife through the edgy region. Some reported sightings of suspicious characters, while others charged that plant security had been inadequate. Still others recalled having seen men smoking about the plant grounds despite stringent precautions. Suspicions of sabotage filled the air. The fears were not without justification. The *Times* recounted on the sixth that the plant had been infiltrated by a German who obtained employment, smuggled matches into the plant and then attempted to commit suicide by blowing up the facility as he placed a match on a loaded shell. The would-be saboteur was subdued, promptly brought to trial and sentenced to a lengthy jail term. Memories of Black Tom, the Jersey City explosion that was only fourteen months in the past, were anxiously recalled and made residents skittish. The comparisons were fueled by reporters who accompanied their press accounts of Gillespie with sidebars about the July 1916 event. However, the entry of the United States into the war created circumstances that marred the comparison, but wary speakers rarely made that distinction. German agents and saboteurs for the most part had departed. Many of them slipped into Mexico, Germany's would-be ally, as they were mindful that sabotage in the time of war was punishable by death. Fervor against this enemy ran so high that anyone having made a pro-German remark at best came under scrutiny and, at worst, suspicion or abuse.

The workforce was also suspect. The jobs were largely unskilled positions in a dangerous activity for which no one had experience. While the aforementioned shell-loading school was on the premises, it trained inspectors, not workers. The government constantly stressed safety, and the fatality rate prior to the explosion was actually very low, but the slightest slip-up could be disastrous. Thus, it was not surprising that Gillespie authorities were promptly able to attribute worker error as the cause of the explosion and explain the event in detail. Indeed, death accompanied the early cleanup. After Edward J. Schenck caused an explosion by the careless striking of a loaded shell on December 17, 1918, flying pieces struck him on the head and chest. While he was able to finish his shift and return to Long Branch that evening, the *Matawan Journal* reported two days later that he died at night shortly after crying out.

The federal government did not possess a disaster relief program in 1918, nor by today's standards did the government quickly pay for the damages caused by its agent Gillespie. There was no Federal Emergency Management Agency (FEMA) to provide speedy and often generous assistance. Another handicap to recovery was the absence of explosion coverage from most business and personal property insurance policies. While the Red Cross and other aid providers were able to offer limited emergency assistance, their help was generally limited to making minimally damaged homes habitable. Part of their repair service was funded by a $100,000 advance by T.A. Gillespie, who perceived that making prompt repairs where needed most would prevent greater damage due to buildings now exposed to the elements. The thousands of claims filed with the federal government required acts of Congress to accept and fund. The slow-moving process was delayed by investigations to separate the legitimate claims from those that were not. The federal justice system may have thought the payments to be an act of generosity. The *Letter from the Secretary of the Treasury*, which submitted some of the claims to Congress, had an opinion appended from E.A. Kreger, the acting judge advocate general, which denied government liability, not only because the government is generally not liable at tort but also, he asserted, because the government's indemnity of Gillespie was solely for the benefit of the latter and there was no evidence that the firm was negligent or liable. He added that construction of a building not in compliance with the laws of New Jersey was not in itself negligence. Thus, the Justice Department indicated that the government was paying claims voluntarily.

The Great War ended only forty-seven days after Gillespie blew up. While the Allied armies made great advances in October, the end of hostilities was sudden if not unexpected, but as the peace negotiations devolved to settle on making the eleventh hour of the eleventh day of the eleventh month the time for the war's end, scattered fighting continued. Some even thought the peace overtures were more ruse than plan. As a consequence, aggressive commanders continued their advances on the morning of the planned armistice, futile gestures that led to the needless waste of lives. Others thought ending the fight was premature, but the forging of peace, like the onset of the war, is beyond the scope of this work. Note in closing, however, that the displeased Pershing, who thought the armistice was a mistake, would later growl, "If they had given us another ten days, we would have rounded up the entire German army, captured it, humiliated it." The British and French, their armies having used their last reserves, did not agree. In addition, wary politicians feared a prostrate Germany might be prone to a Bolshevist revolution.[9]

6

THE MORGAN STORAGE DEPOT

The end of war brought about a transformation of the sprawling government facility at Morgan. The changes resulted in profound economic, social and political impact, much of which was not for the better.

The easy decision to halt immediately reconstruction of the shell-loading plant was made in an instant. Other loading plants continued production for brief periods due to the government's need to terminate contracts, but the much greater challenge was the return from Europe of enormous stores of military supplies and weapons. Demobilization soon transformed Morgan into an enormous storage depot. The selection of the site, along with several others in the East, was made for a practical reason: its proximity to eastern seacoast ports.

The T.A. Gillespie Shell Loading Company of Morgan ceased activity as a government manufacturing entity in early 1919, the same time the government placed the operation of the plant in the new organization known as the Morgan General Ordnance Depot. It was a gradual process, as suggested by a brief *Citizen* item on December 21, "One by one the different units of the Morgan plant are being taken over by the Ordnance Department. It is expected that by early next week practically every T.A. Gillespie man will be off the plant." The transfer was planned to be effective on or about February 1, 1919, according to interviews with Robert E. Eldridge that were summarized in the *Matawan Journal* on January 9, 1919. Eldridge also noted that eighteen carloads of munitions that had been recently received at Morgan were defective shells recently stored at Craigens Brick Yard in

Cliffwood, which were intended to be either dumped at sea or sent to arsenals in Fort Wingate, New Mexico, or Charleston, South Carolina. The latter was also to receive shells in perfect condition, while unused raw materials, including TNT, ammonium nitrate and amatol, were intended to go to the former. Eldridge maintained that only non-explosive materials would be stored at Morgan. Captain Watson of the Ordnance Department added that while many rumors were circulating about the planned arsenal, he believed that stored equipment would be vehicles and supplies, also claiming that "he was certain that the Secretary of War's declaration that no explosives would be stored there still holds and would for all time." Eldridge also addressed the recent reconstruction efforts, noting that only the administrative offices, restaurants and barracks had been rebuilt prior to the armistice.

Congressman Thomas J. Scully lived in South Amboy, so his interest in issues of safety and compensation was both local and personal. He had earlier assurances from Benedict Crowell, the assistant secretary of war, that storage there of TNT was "substantially reduced" and that the department had under "consideration" a plan for handling explosives at points contiguous to thickly populated sections. Scully said he had "positive assurance from the War Department that all T.N.T. is being removed from the State of New Jersey."[1] Confirmation of the aforementioned dumping at sea activity by a brief *Citizen* account on December 21 was intended to assuage residents' wariness by the claim that the action meant that local safety took precedence over the potential lost value of salvage. Whatever the initial assurances were to allay the fears of the public, they proved puffery through the later realization that there continued to be a major munitions presence at Gillespie. On the other hand, the dropping of munitions to the bottom of the bay, while there existed an oyster fishery no less, hardly seems to be a safety precaution in this era of sensitive treatment of the environment. While no issue over ordnance dumped in Raritan Bay appears to have surfaced, one can be wary of how long term the potential hazard is when considering a Delaware case in which loads of clam shells recovered for crushing and laying for driveway surfaces were found to contain World War I ordnance dumped off that state. The recovered material included many grenades and a small number of mustard gas shells, one of the notorious poison weapons of that war.

While the remarks of Eldridge and the congressman's assurances from the secretary of war have a mitigating tone, conditions at Morgan were anything but. The greatest mystery in the Gillespie clearance and salvage period is the continued presence of munitions, specifically how much was stored and for how long. The Middlesex County Board of Chosen Freeholders sought to investigate in early 1919 why explosives needed to be stored in the region. Its naivety to military necessity would turn its "why" into "how much." Its concern would lead to the regular review of reports on the subject, an insight inferred from news items such as a *Citizens* news account of its recent meeting, published on December 13:

> *A report from the property officer at the Morgan General Ordnance Depot for the week ending November 29, was read, showing that during preceding week 8,285 high explosive shells had been shipped, leaving a balance on hand as of the 29th of 425,977. Other explosives stored at the reservation were reported as follows: Low explosive shells, 1,745,063; smokeless powder, 443,455.75 pounds, amatol, 197,046 pounds; T.N.T. 6,662 pounds and tetryl, 1,050 pounds.*

It was likely always wary and watchful. Perhaps it expected the grounds to have been cleared three and a half years later when it made an inspection trip to Morgan and "uncovered" 180,000 pounds of black powder and 375,000 boosters. A year would pass before it was all removed. Another form of nonlethal salvage was unfilled shells, presumably removed by the military early in the cleanup. Some of them found their way to fabricators, which made Morgan souvenir lamps and ashtrays.

The other area plants were also in the process of change. The government takeover of the Gillespie affiliate California Loading has provided the best insight into its activity. *The Iron Age* of March 6, 1919, reported,

> *Effective March 1, the Ordnance Department has taken over the shell loading plant of the California Loading Co., Old Bridge, N.J., to be used as an arsenal and storage depot. The plant occupies a site of about 175 acres of land with an aggregate of over 40 buildings for shell production, with addition of electric light and power plant for works operation, three sawmills and other miscellaneous structures. Construction of the plant was inaugurated about April 15, 1918 and before the close of the war 200,000 loaded shells were manufactured. The works are said to have cost over $1,500,000, with employment at one time given to close to 2,000 persons. A portion of the plant is now being used for regular shell loading work, and it is understood will be so operated for some months to come. R.L. Oliver, associated with the Oliver Loading Co., is vice-president and managing director.*

Reports of accidents also served as revelations of remaining ordnance. On June 13, 1922, Arthur Scully was using a hammer and chisel on machinery when he created a spark that caused an explosion, requiring his hospitalization for the treatment of burns and sending six shells flying a great distance. Finally, in November 1923, the plant superintendent, Reuben Forgotson, announced that the Morgan depot was free of explosives. By that time, the government was genuinely motivated to clean up the place as it planned to sell it.

Eldridge also addressed a fear that the local community had begun to experience: an enormous loss of employment. Even non-working householders felt the impact, as "Rooms to Let" signs popped up all over South Amboy, a place where

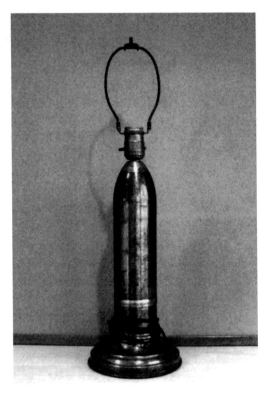

An enormous number of unfilled, undamaged shell casings were leftover after the armistice. Memento lamps were made from Gillespie unloaded shells. *Courtesy of Thomas Warne Museum.*

in the recent past it had been impossible to find a spare room. Local hope and anticipation for the post-government era lent themselves to periodic rumors about major prospective commercial use. Early ones included a 1920 report that Henry Ford was interested in the property or Baldwin Locomotives the next year per the *South Amboy Citizen* of January 20, 1920, and April 9, 1921, respectively.

The great force of guards and materials handlers meant there would be a lot of men with time on their hands at Morgan. The Camp Morgan YMCA was active early on in providing social and recreational outlets, and a Gillespie team continued to compete in 1919 in the local industrial baseball league. However, to the consternation of the local populace, too many found their way to town. The First Baptist Church approached the matter delicately in January when it pointed out that the "increasing number of soldiers from Morgan seen on our streets at night, and the boldness of a very few, is causing some easiness among our women folks when obliged go leave their homes without an escort after dark." After pointing out that the great post-explosion strain suffered by the local women might have heightened sensitivities, they suggested that military police patrol the streets. The city council's pleas for help were blunt in a petition for help: "Whereas these troops have given the city police force considerable trouble," it was a force that was inadequate in its numbers.

The government maintained the Morgan Depot for several years, but historical knowledge of activity there appears limited to a relative handful of news accounts, although a long series of pictures taken in 1919, which accompany this section, provides good evidence of the automobile storage area. The pictures also indicate the nature of plant construction in general. One major challenge that proved an ongoing concern, even problem, was guarding the plant. The experienced Gillespie guards who were discharged beginning on December 17, 1918, were replaced by ordnance depot soldiers, an arrangement less than satisfactory. However, some Gillespie guards appear to have been inducted into the army for service there. Reports of inadequate protection or poorly behaved guards were repeated over the next two years. The City of South Amboy soon urged that military police help protect the city. By March, civilian guards were employed as military men sought to leave this assignment. Perhaps the greatest potential risk of inadequate protection was a report by the South Amboy port warden in February that claimed a scow loaded with explosives was laid up unprotected for over twenty-four hours. The city council speculated on what considerable harm could have been done in those circumstances by one with evil intent. On the other hand, a report in May that the civilian guard payroll was over $100,000 monthly was meant to impress that the facility was well protected.

The motor vehicle storage facility was among the most significant of the depot's functions. As the *South Amboy Citizen* noted on May 17, 1919, "Great trains of government-owned trucks still continue to run though this city [South Amboy] to the storage ground at Camp Morgan." The *Newark Evening News* described in depth this extensive, carefully planned vehicle operation. Its account was reprinted by the *South Amboy Citizen* on December 6, 1919. There were about two thousand trucks in storage, each jacked up off the ground, while parts susceptible to rust and cylinders were well covered with oil. They also had over 150 motorcycles, many sidecars, about 1,200 bicycles, 900 ambulance bodies and 300 ambulance chases. The aforementioned "great trains of trucks" had come from Kearny, where they had stopped at the armistice while en route to ports of embarkation. The storage depot consisted of "thirty-one buildings. Some of them are of wooden mill construction sheathed with sheet iron. Others are steel-truss sectional buildings of the 'knock-down' variety. Others are part brick and part wood. All are immense, substantial, adequate to their purpose." The explosion left some partially remaining brick walls, which Major J.S. Crane of the Quartermaster Construction Corps used for foundations of some buildings at a fraction of the cost of new construction. "He carried these walls up to the required height of twenty feet or so with wood construction, put on his roofs and there you are."

These vehicles and others were disposed of in time. Sales had been ongoing up to the following February, when an announcement of a public auction scheduled for February 27, 1920, was uncovered from the *Citizen*. It indicated that the vehicles on the block would include Ford delivery, roadster and touring cars, Autocar trucks, Selden trucks and Studebaker three-quarter-ton trucks, among others. The army was apparently interested in retaining some vehicles but was unable to measure future need until Congress determined the size of the future standing regular forces. Transportation at Morgan would be in the thoughts of public-minded locals for another reason: their realization that employment at the former Gillespie's would

Plant storage buildings were typically long, narrow structures of temporary construction. This may be the largest—a reported two hundred feet. *Courtesy of Special Collections and University Archives, Rutgers University.*

The return of a great number of military vehicles from France, along with munitions, necessitated the construction of a storage terminal and resulted in a new incarnation for part of the Gillespie grounds. *Courtesy of Special Collections and University Archives, Rutgers University.*

A long series of pictures for the construction of the postwar storage facility survives, although at times it is not evident if the image is the repair of a Gillespie plant building or new construction. This illustration shows a typical building type, corrugated steel over a steel frame. *Courtesy of Special Collections and University Archives, Rutgers University.*

Other buildings were built over wood frames. Heavy wood beams, eight by eight or larger, are more resistant to destruction from fire than steel. *Courtesy of Special Collections and University Archives, Rutgers University.*

The presence of two-story buildings indicates that a small part of the loading facility was not destroyed. The second story was used for the mixing and heating of amatol. The scene is an unspecified location. *Courtesy of Special Collections and University Archives, Rutgers University.*

The explosion left some partially remaining brick walls, which Major J.S. Crane of the Quartermaster Construction Corps used for foundations of some buildings at a fraction of the cost of new construction. He then built these walls up to the required height of twenty feet with wood. *Special Collections and University Archives, Rutgers University.*

end. The actual planning for a transportation facility would involve the water's surface. A scenario unbelievable nearly a century later seems then to have been harebrained in its concept and hopelessly retrograde in its planning. Local public and business leaders sought construction of a canal to begin at Cheesequake Creek and cut across the state to the Delaware River. Their efforts were utterly futile.

The advertisements by house-wrecking companies for the sale of salvageable building materials that appeared regularly in the local press in the early 1920s suggested how wrecked buildings were being removed.

OTHER EXPLOSIONS

Middlesex County continued to be a danger zone after the war as long after the armistice explosions continued to kill and maim across the county. Even the Gillespie plant's new incarnation as a storage depot did not eliminate the hazards and dangers of handling munitions there. In addition, sudden death could loom from major and minor eruptions, from known areas of risk and from unexpected sources, not only at Gillespie's but also elsewhere in the county. Middlesex residents would have been justified if they had believed that hostilities were still not over in the summer of 1919. That year, the potential for widespread disaster became plainly and painfully evident at Camp Raritan. As background, this 3,200-acre facility in Edison Township, which was then Raritan Township, opened in 1917, when it was built for the most part as a storage facility for weapons subsequently shipped overseas. The word "Arsenal" was added to the facility's name the following year. Following the end of the war, Raritan Arsenal, still alternately known as Camp Raritan, was made a permanent installation.

The construction of Raritan at all was accomplished only after overcoming daunting challenges in its inhospitable environment. Although the locale possessed the prime assets of proximity to deep water and rail connections, the wet nature of the land at this construction site was a strict liability. Engineers built a dike nine miles long around the entire reservation in order to contain extensive salt marshes, which flooded with each high tide. Piles had to be driven through the frozen ground during the harsh 1917–18 winter, as poor soil conditions required additional support for the buildings.[2] After the war's end, the arsenal became a major recovery, processing and transfer point for vehicles and weapons returned from Europe. Vast quantities of munitions were stored there. Then, disaster struck. On August 4, 1919, two box cars of TNT blew up, resulting in a fire that caused a secondary explosion in a magazine. Excitement and fear spread as firemen fought to contain the blaze. Although initial reports suggested fatalities might have been avoided, hopes were dashed as the death toll reached nine. The fears of local residents were captured by the *Matawan Journal* headline on the seventh, which also reflected the potential of the near-disaster "Similar to the One at Morgan Last October."

The fears from remaining munitions activities, buried shells and explosions from a variety of causes were long lasting in Morgan and the surrounding region. The litany of deaths from munitions explosions in the post–World War I period in Middlesex County and nearby areas underscores the hazards of their storage, transport and unexpected discovery in the ground and elsewhere. One such early example in Sayreville involved workers who, on September 29, 1921, were in the process of removing old pipe at the Parlin DuPont plant. As they believed that one pipe was filled with dirt, they struck it in an attempt to dislodge the material, but the pipe's contents was guncotton that remained from an old manufacturing operation. The resultant explosion killed seven and reverberated with a widely felt shock that also revived memories of Morgan.

The handling of salvaged weapons was an inherently dangerous operation that took the life of Francis Holton on March 7, 1922. The popular twenty-one-year-old had been dismantling shells purchased by the Columbia Salvage Company when one exploded, sending shrapnel through his head and arm. The good wages of loading were apparently a casualty of peace. The tone of the *South Amboy Citizen* reporter on the eleventh was anger laden as he hinted of inadequate training while pointing out that wages were merely a "measly" $0.32 cents hourly, or $2.56 per day.

Two years later, the Atlas Powder Company was in the process of transferring defective powder from Charleston, South Carolina, to Lake Hopatcong, New Jersey, via the Pennsylvania Railroad's powder dock at South Amboy. Some observers noticed that boxcars were ablaze on its trestle and attempted to minimize damage by removing the burning cars. A sudden explosion at 7:13 p.m. on September 6, 1923, rained burning powder on passersby and motorists who had stopped to watch the removal and also destroyed a number of automobiles. The engineer of a passenger train, who at first thought he could slowly pass by the fire, had the presence of mind to halt just yards in front of the explosion. Following the blast, his terrified passengers scattered in panic. After four barges located nearby caught fire, they were towed into Raritan Bay, where they were allowed to burn and sink. As the night wore on, the authorities were fearful that damaged light poles raised the risk of falling wires, so they turned off electrical power. South Amboy was cast into darkness. The death toll reached five, while scores were injured. As fear-stricken residents watched the spreading fire, memories of the Gillespie terror were again rekindled. Fortunately, the fears proved unfounded.

An act of God caused the heaviest toll in New Jersey from a military explosion between the world wars, but the consequences of the explosion and spreading fires were similar to those at Gillespie. The United States Naval Ammunition Depot at Lake Denmark, Rockaway Township, Morris County, was struck by lightning on July 10, 1926. Storehouse Number 8, which contained 670,000 pounds of explosives, was hit. The resultant initial explosion set off fires and a series of secondary explosions that totally destroyed everything within three thousand feet of the initial blast, causing extensive property damage over a wide area, including adjacent Picatinny Arsenal, and killing nineteen people. By a stroke of mitigating fortune, the explosion occurred on a Saturday afternoon when only a light workforce was on the site, a chance of timing that prevented many additional deaths.

The scene of the resultant devastation there was not unlike that at Gillespie. The ground was littered with collapsed and burned buildings, twisted metal that had been rail lines and unexploded ordnance. The physical layout at the two places shared one shortcoming: the separation of stored explosives. Safety standards for industry, as well as the military, evolve from lessons learned from accidents. Separation was at a greater distance at Lake Denmark than at Gillespie, but the distance met only federal standards rather than the stricter ones established by the State of New Jersey. Since this accident was on a permanent military installation, the subsequent military investigation had long-reaching consequences. The investigators found that conditions existed at other ammunition depots that could make them subject to similar loss. Their studies led to new safety standards and the establishment of the Department of Defense Explosives Safety Board.

The explosion predictably raised alarm among the public and elected officials, who agitated for stricter controls and the reduction of munitions storage in populated areas. As a consequence, over the next few years explosives were removed from Raritan Arsenal, an area where local protests had begun years prior to Lake Denmark.

The discovery of buried ordnance at home made living in proximity to Gillespie an enduring domestic risk. The hazard was uncovered in the yard of the Ernest Reed family at 374 Prospect Street, South Amboy, on March 24, 1930, as was reported by the *South Amboy Citizen* seven days later. As the Reed children burned leaves and debris, the fire reached a buried 75mm shell, which exploded. While the children escaped injury, the Reed home and the two adjoining residences were damaged.

The risk of death visited some who were unaware that they were handling munitions. Death by explosion was the fate of Raymond Cox, a home craftsman who had been hammering to shape for other use a piece of iron that he found on the beach. Unaware that it contained explosives, he was killed instantly on August 29, 1925, when it exploded.

At times, the injured may or may not have been aware but simply forgot. Enrico Fioretti, when at Morgan in 1921 to get a truckload of dirt, noticed a number of shells lying around, so he took them as souvenirs, believing they were duds. The shells were again lying around for years, this time in his backyard at 122 Liberty Street in Fords. One exploded on August 14, 1937,

In 1930, a shell exploded at 374 Prospect Street, South Amboy, while leaves were being burned. It was a forerunner of the emerging domestic hazards.

Closely packed cabins were a longtime summer respite for vacationers at Morgan Beach.
Courtesy of Special Collections and University Archives, Rutgers University.

when the Fiorettis were cooking tomatoes over an open flame. The pair was seriously injured by the resultant explosion.

Life in Morgan, Sayreville and the Raritan River area of Middlesex County would, in time, return to normality after the war, but the process of adjustment took longer in view of the aforementioned hazards of explosives. In addition, residents needed to learn to live with the long-term presence of the Morgan storage depot and terminal. Morgan Beach, actually on the south shore or Old Bridge side of Cheesequake Creek, remained the locus of a summer colony of closely packed cabin dwellers. As the 1920s unfolded, the nearby bayshore would be extensively developed with small summer cottages on tiny lots. Bay View Manor, which the Steuerwalds so enthusiastically promoted shortly prior to the explosion, remained largely undeveloped until after World War II. Its promoters, Charles L. and Ethel B., relocated in 1928 to Middletown, where they bought one of the older houses in the township's ancient Middletown Village historic district. The environment was pleasant and safe, a notable contrast to life on the edge of a munitions plant.

A Proposed Canal and Political Wrangling

As background to the canal proposal, recall that the expansion of South Amboy as a rail center in the third quarter of the nineteenth century motivated its governing body to shed much of its territory. The then township sought to retain its railroad-generated tax revenues in a smaller, concentrated territory, but later it not only lacked area in which to grow but also learned that a transportation facility was planned just outside its borders, thereby passing South Amboy. Thereafter, South Amboy made repeated efforts to secure the return of part of adjoining Sayreville, including Morgan. While the intrigue of municipal politics is beyond the ambit of this book, their last effort in the postwar recovery period merits closer examination. South Amboy, which in 1908 changed its municipal organization to a city, maintained that Melrose and Morgan, including Bay View Manor, were a "natural part" of their city due to proximity and their distance from the more settled parts of Sayreville. While that was true from a geographical perspective, and those parts of Sayreville often felt like forgotten appendages, they belonged to the latter, which had no intention of surrendering them. The road from the southern end of the county bridge in Sayreville passed through South Amboy streets before resuming its course within Sayreville's sparsely settled Morgan before entering Old Bridge and continuing toward the shore. To meet the demands of increasing traffic, the state built a new segment of highway east of South Pine Avenue in the mid-1920s, a link in the eventual Route 35, which made the separation of the two aforementioned sections even more pronounced. Melrose appeared to have been cleaved with an axe. South Amboy's designs on its previously ceded land stem from the plans for that bridge.

The rail line into South Amboy had been the only land crossing prior to the construction of the bridge, which had been first rumored in 1892. When the site selected in 1894 turned out to be in Sayreville, South Amboy strove to recover its old territory but was rebuffed. Later, the proposed annexation bill died in committee in 1910, while another annexation attempt in 1919 was rejected. The latter has been cited as the last attempt by South Amboy to regain part of Sayreville.[3] However, South Amboy would renew its designs on Morgan in the 1920s, when motivated for another transportation-related reason. Local political and real estate figures had renewed efforts to secure construction of a cross–New Jersey ship canal, not only an idea that had come and passed but also one that most observers would have thought was buried. The revived plan would begin at Cheesequake Creek and end in the

Delaware River around Bordentown, where its southerly route would take it past the major port of Philadelphia.

Two canals were cut across New Jersey in the nineteenth century at a time when an effective cross-state means for the transit of goods was vital. The utility of canals was soon surpassed by the railroads, which effectively made the canals obsolete for most of their existence. The Delaware & Raritan Canal, completed in 1834, had been waning for many years prior to its 1932 demise. Similarly, the Morris Canal, opened in 1831, staggered along at the end before its 1924 closing. Since coal was the primary fuel for heating and the generation of electricity, the promoters could attempt to furnish economic justification for the canal. The Intracoastal Waterway was the principal shore-water transit project during the era. It was a network from New England to Florida that utilized existing coastal inlets and bays and newly constructed courses and canals to provide smaller craft a partially protected route along the frequently treacherous Atlantic seaboard. The cross–New Jersey plan would have eliminated the New Jersey coastal section, which begins in the area around Barnegat. The tendency for underestimating construction and maintenance costs, along with overly optimistic traffic and revenue projections, is beyond the ambit of this work. However, the political intrigue and the plans to remake part of the Gillespie grounds make the canal crucial to the narrative, especially as the government planned its sale.

The *Citizen* editorialized on December 25, 1920, for annexation "on lines of mutual concession to right and justice," which in their view would mean an advantage for South Amboy. When the lack of water made a 1921 fire in the Melrose section adjacent to South Amboy difficult to control, South Amboy pointed out in an effort to influence residents there that the city's water would have been of great value. The South Amboy mayor's message early in 1923 indicated that additional territory was of vital necessity, but to his city, of course. In 1923, South Amboy advertised its intent to seek an annexation bill for the legislature, but nothing happened. The background of the boundary issue was the desire to secure the site for the Raritan end of the canal. The canal proposal also experienced difficulty in an effort to gain traction, making a case for its prospect savings in transportation costs compared with construction costs. The cause received a damaging blow from a 1930 army report, which questioned the cost subject. The issue, only briefly highlighted here, would appear to have been hopeless. Perhaps the perception of its end was perceived by the buyers of the Gillespie tract who held it for only a brief period. Sayreville remained intact.

The section of the plant that had been acquired by Gillespie as agent for the government was transferred to the United States on June 10, 1921, and then by the United States on April 5, 1924, to local investors, who included the Perth Amboy real estate figure Isaac Alpern and manufacturer Sigmund Eisner. Eisner, the world's largest producer of uniforms, was headquartered in Red Bank but opened a branch factory in South Amboy during the war. Preparation of the grounds by the government appears to have focused on the removal of munitions and military equipment, a revelation by Fred C. Hermann, owner of the Van Brunt & Son transportation company that was successor to an ancient Matawan stagecoach line. In a letter dated March 26, 1983, now in the possession of the Thomas Warne Museum of the Madison Township Historical Society, Hermann recalled some great memories of his youth:

> *In 1925 my father was in charge of a project to clean up the old barracks and government material left over from the war. A group of investors including Morgan Larson, Abe Jelin and others hired him to gather the surplus and sell it. He had about 50 or so men working for him and we lived in what was then the old officers' headquarters and which is now a small factory on Highway 35 in Morgan.*

The real interest of the investors was for the potential commercial value of the land. The buyers' thoughts were linked to the historic role of South Amboy as a transportation center, but their ambitions were greater, as revealed by the *Matawan Journal* on July 13, 1923. The group planned to utilize the salvageable buildings for the government depot period as a storage and shipment center for southern and western manufacturers. This account indicated the availability of forty-three iron buildings with a capacity of 1 million square feet and numerous other buildings on a plot described earlier as 1,433 acres. Their development hinged on the aforementioned conversion of Cheesequake Creek into a shipping canal, one that could handle oceangoing vessels, along with a more attainable dredging of a channel to Sandy Hook. The thwarted plans for the canal would make their interest in the Gillespie grounds short-term.

Morgan attained a large and popular dining-drinking and recreational following, especially given its small area, as it became a stopping point for those destined for the shore. Many travelers chose to stop, notably the ones who opted to partake of a repast at the traditional Ye Old Spye Inn or the new Cady's. J.H. Cady, who had earlier operated a small restaurant near

One can still contemplate lighters using Cheesequake Creek, a once active, local commercial waterway. However, a canal for oceangoing vessels would have disrupted road and rail travel, as well as negatively impacted the environment. The railroad bridge, open in the background, would have been only one impediment.

the railroad crossing, opened his House of Seafood on the bay adjoining Cheesequake Creek on April 22, 1926. The large establishment that seated two hundred reflected the optimism of the times and aimed to draw the growing traffic on the future Highway 35. The place, later renamed the Robert E. Lee Inn, endured for six decades. However, many more motorists stopped unwillingly when stalled at its drawbridge over Cheesequake Creek, which became a notorious bottleneck and source of massive traffic jams.

The first destination south of Morgan was Laurence Harbor, located in the northeasterly section of Old Bridge. The area had an auspicious beginning when established as the country estate of Laurence Lamb, who also founded the Laurence Harbor Golf and Country Club and built a clubhouse designed by James Brown Lord. The place's twentieth-century incarnation, however, would be an area divided into small lots built with small summer homes. Cliffwood Beach in Aberdeen Township lacked the pedigree of a country club but shared the early twentieth-century development pattern of inexpensive summer accommodations for northern New Jersey city dwellers. The most prominent bayshore developers were Morrisey & Walker, a firm headquartered in Keansburg that was founded

PHONE 460 SOUTH AMBOY

Nᵒ 2529   MORGAN TERMINAL COMPANY

AT CAMP MORGAN, N. J.

SHIPPING ORDER

DATE

SHIP BY

REMARKS

The billhead from the sale of a truck to a private citizen in 1926 indicates a continuing disposal operation, this around the time of the Morrissey & Walker purchase the same year. Camp Morgan was an informal name for the grounds.

in 1915. They built a boardwalk and beach facilities, which enabled them to attract a wide following. The savvy promoters built Treasure Lake and utilized a pirate theme in their advertising building, which included a replica of a pirate ship serving as their Highway 35 office. The ship became a widely known bayshore landmark that was eagerly looked for by impatient youthful automobile passengers who knew that once you saw the pirate ship, you were almost there. I remember. Thus, the firm was well positioned to prosper from the 1920s growth of automobile excursions.

Morrisey & Walker would have secured a major success and elevated the stature of its bayshore business if its optimistic projections at the June 1926 purchase of the plant had been fulfilled. It organized the Morgan Development and Investment Company, which obtained fine pre-purchase coverage in the *Times* of March 6, which depicted the land as one of the largest undeveloped shore tracts close to New York, near the Laurence Harbor beach on Raritan Bay, while also well situated with respect to roads and rail lines. It was reported as planning to build roads and recreation parks to make it suitable for a resort center but was undecided in its division either into small estates from one to three acres or into lots with a maximum frontage of fifty feet. The sale of material continued as indicated by the June 17 billhead representing the sale of a Mack truck.

Sayreville's success in building its industrial base made genuine the town's promotional slogan: "Home of Nationally Known Industries." The National Lead Company, makers of Dutch Boy Paint, arrived by around 1930, a substantial addition to the aforementioned DuPont and Hercules. They formed an industrial "big three," which, along with the brick firms, virtually guaranteed employment to any able-bodied man who sought a manufacturing job. Joseph T. Karcher, Sayreville promoter par-excellent, claimed that his personal initiative helped bring the firm to Sayreville after it was reported to have been considering a location at a nearby town. National Lead, which built an enormous complex on

The former Sayre & Fisher power plant is an above-the-ground reminder of its former presence. The firm's facility was the initial provider of electric power to the town.

the Raritan River on property bought from Sayre & Fisher, was a major employer for over half a century.[4]

The town's ability to attract industry continued for decades, which reinforced and made real a second town boast that "Industries Prefer Sayreville." The factories created an enormous base of industrial ratables that consistently enabled Sayreville to keep its municipal tax rate low. Indeed, for years, Sayreville did not have a municipal property tax, a status that was of great appeal to prospective and existing homeowners. Sayreville in the years between the wars was home to a growing population that lived in modest houses, shopped locally and maintained strong neighborhood identities.

The element of time was not propitious for the Morgan Development and Investment Company. Its parent organization, Morrisey & Walker, as noted, already had extensive holdings in the nearby towns of Laurence Harbor in Old Bridge Township, Cliffwood Beach in Aberdeen Township, Keansburg and farther south in Shark River Hills in Neptune Township. The firm specialized in small, relatively inexpensive lots that were typically bought by city-dwellers who built summer homes. Each of the foregoing areas was closer to the bayshore and laid out in lots ready to sell and build. In addition, the land had little appeal for private estates. The Raritan was not an appealing beach, while the ocean shore and environs, not that far distant, were by then the favored choice of the landed gentry.

Morrisey & Walker's proposed development of the Gillespie grounds did not materialize for reasons that are readily inferred. The firm continued sales activity in the aforementioned communities through the late 1920s, but even these transactions came to a virtual halt when the Great Depression sent the real estate market into a tailspin. That national economic cataclysm both put an end to area real estate business and sent many of the Morrisey & Walker and similar ilk properties into arrears. For additional woe, their municipalities were plagued by the resultant tax sales. Differences during these rough times resulted in an enduring rift between the partners. The Gillespie grounds would remain barren for the most part until the demands of a growing Sayreville determined that the area was developable.

7

THE REGION AFTER WORLD WAR II

The plant grounds after the munitions cleanup in time turned into a desolate landscape, and so it remained for decades. The earliest-known aerial photographs taken in the 1930s show its scarred expanse, crossed by a web of former plant roads spread over this vast area that became an abandoned wilderness. The grounds remained in that condition absent any reason to be changed or developed. However, one of Gillespie's roads emerged into public use. In 1936, the plant's principal east–west thoroughfare was acquired by Sayreville from Morgan Development and Investment Company and Whitehead Bros. Company. Although the borough council officially named the now public way the Ernston Road Extension, many locals referred to the newly opened street by its traditional moniker, "Old Morgan Plant Road," and continued to do so for decades.[1]

Elsewhere in Sayreville, Presidents Park became the new name for the Ernston section in recognition of a 1926 development north of Washington Road. The area was filled in after the war with enlarged Cape Cod houses.

Steuerwald sold numerous Bay View Manor lots around the time Gillespie was being built, but this area at Morgan's eastern edge became built up only after World War II. George Wist, who after World War II bought a Liberty Street lot that the borough acquired after a tax sale, recalled in a 2010 interview with the Sayreville Historical Society how undeveloped Bay View Manor was. After building a two-car garage, his family lived in it until he could complete the house. He claimed there were hardly any houses when he began and that the houses there were not built until the 1950s.

For years, the grounds of the Gillespie plant were an abandoned wasteland. *Courtesy of Sayreville Historical Society.*

The character of the former Gillespie tract was suggested by one commentator who pointed out in anonymity that it was "just a packed dirt area with makeshift roads that locals made to use to drive around on." This person indicated that she and the other kids learned to drive there before attaining legal age. Others hunted small game. Adventuresome boys found playing grounds, if not fields, there.

Everett Mercer related his memories of the time to me:

As a young boy in the 1950s, my dad would take me hunting for rabbits with our beagles. Often, the dogs would kick up a rabbit in the woods, and the rabbit would run to hide under one of the old building foundations. I recall distinctly there were building remains and underground bunkers on both sides of the Parkway and both sides of Ernston Road, or the Old Morgan Plant Road, as we called it. The old roads were partly overgrown but discernible, and both my father, Rip Mercer, and Uncle Bill Inman would train the dogs in the fall by just walking the old roads. The construction of the Parkway really divided the property and destroyed many of the old foundations. I also recall foundations as far west as the site of the London Terrace Apartments on the south side of Ernston Road, east of

Route 9. I also remember finding old clay and wooden drain pipes in the vicinity of Oak View Nursing Home on Ernston Road, which were used those to prevent "sparking" if gunpowder spilled into floor drains. When you consider all the old materials that were around, I wouldn't say that any part of the grounds were cleared.

Ken Elyea recalled finding a dangerous situation in the area in the 1950s:

We were playing in a lightly wooded area near Ernston Road about a quarter mile west of the Parkway and found on the surface of the grounds a couple of buried brick structures. They were deep, wider at the bottom and narrow at the top. It was scary because they were uncovered, and if you fell in, there was no way out. I later realized from the shape that they were magazines, which were typically constructed that way so the force of an accidental blast would go upwards.

Part of the region became a dump. As Peter McIntyre reflected on the late 1950s and 1960s:

The area from the Parkway bridges over Ernston Road on both sides of Ernston was a dumping ground for old cars, appliances and every type of household refuse. We kids thought these piles of trash were treasure chests. The area along the road from Ernston to the creek—it's now Gondek Drive—west to the Parkway was a hill which we saw leveled by the truckload, fill dirt just taken away. Here was where we found old shells. The discovery of a shell was not a big deal. I saw many of them in those years. The soil on the other side of the Parkway where Eisenhower School was built was so soft and sandy that we called it "the desert" and played around there.

A nationwide change in travel and residential patterns would help transform Sayreville in the post–World War II period. The mass movement of people out of the cities into outlying areas was propelled by the millions of servicemen resuming civilian life, a housing shortage that required a prompt remedy, low-cost government-guaranteed loans and highway construction policies that opened new vistas in once-distant territory. Sayreville became immediately appealing as the first destination on the state highways south of the Raritan River. The evolving trend accelerated after the opening of the Garden State Parkway, a superhighway that spanned the entire easterly

Left: Shells remaining from Gillespie have been found over the area for years; many were retained as souvenirs. Others undoubtedly remain in the ground. *Courtesy of John Ruszala.*

Below: The housing boom in post–World War II Sayreville eventually made the Gillespie grounds desirable for new construction, a trend detectable by comparing the two aerial images.

section of the state. Millions of auto travelers pass through the borough unaware of the locale, as there is no "Entering Sayreville" sign at the southern end of the Parkway's Driscoll Bridge over the Raritan River. The construction of the Garden State Parkway uncovered hazards that foretold potential problems that would plague the former Gillespie region for decades. Earthmoving equipment preparing the new roadbeds uncovered underground pits that required filling. They also found a more startling, fearful hazard of great significance, the aforementioned buried ordnance. Of course, this old ordnance required removal. The discovery was reported by the *Red Bank Register* of March 12, 1953. However, the road builders were faced with an even more vexing challenge in this area. The marshy grounds around Cheesequake Creek were found unable to support the roadway. Innovative techniques for stabilizing the ground needed to be developed and were later employed before this section of the parkway was completed. As part of the project, a small segment of Cheesequake Creek was rerouted near the roadbed. Sayreville had plenty of buildable land, especially as the brick industries were waning. A circa 1960 aerial photograph shows the former Gillespie plant nearly surrounded by new construction.

The new house market in 1950s Sayreville was built to appeal to the borough's traditional blue-collar background but also followed regional and national trends. The new house was satisfactory by the standards of a time when two thousand square feet were considered generous. Builders in Sayreville were not eager to reach for the next emerging price bracket as they would steadily do in newer towns closer to the seashore, but they would change their outlook when a key section of the Gillespie grounds was made ready for construction. When the Kaplan Construction Company built Oak Tree Village north of Ernston Road in the mid-1960s, the size and price of the new Sayreville house went up. The development, which included the site of the 6-1-1 unit that was the first to explode, meant people would live on ground zero. It was also an area that might be expected to have old munitions present. The site of the image on page 72 is near the future Oak Tree Village. The vast number of shells that were collected immediately after the explosion is likely not all that were lodged in the area. The Kaplan construction crews regularly lifted them from the foundation dirt they were removing.

Frank Ludlow, who now lives on the site of the initial explosion, recalled that as a youngster he frequently saw the Kaplan workers stacking shells along the lampposts at the edge of the road and army trucks arriving regularly to remove them. Of course, at the time, discovery of buried ordnance was

While buried ordnance had been regularly uncovered in the area for years, especially during construction of the surrounding housing, when a large shell was found across Eisenhower School on Ernston Road, the matter of possible remaining buried explosive material became a major public issue.

The pleasant Oak Tree Village neighborhood, one filled with fine houses in a quiet, tranquil setting, now makes up the environs of ground zero. Most there in 2012 have no idea of the region's military past.

neither unusual nor the cause of alarm. After Kaplan continued construction on the south side of Ernston Road, the heavy increase in population required a new school. Eisenhower School was built around 1969 on the north side of Ernston Road, west of the Garden State Parkway and on the southern edge of Oak Tree Village, an area an observant child might readily project as contaminated. However, there was no alarm, as uncovering old ordnance had been commonplace for half a century. It remained so until buried munitions were discovered near Eisenhower School.

ORDNANCE REMEDIATION

An artillery shell that measured over nine inches in diameter was found in early August 1994 on Ernston Road, across from Eisenhower School. It prompted the army to conduct a search of 3,100 acres in the vicinity of the Gillespie plant. While great exertions were made to ensure a thorough search in a campaign that raised community attention, if not alarm, the discovery would hardly have been a surprise to those who witnessed or participated in activity there prior to construction of either housing or school. After an extensive investigation that extended in an approximately one-and-a-quarter-mile radius from the site of the explosion, the army conceded that buried ordnance might still be in certain places. Their community meetings and the extensive publicity about their work served to elevate awareness of the event in the immediate area. Michael Zazzarino and Joseph Grabas, who are adults at publication, would hardly have been surprised. When they were youths at about the time the school was under construction, they found an old shell on Scheid Drive opposite the site of the school. Michael regarded the shell as a trophy of play and spent a protracted period knocking clay off the prize. Joseph recalled that the discovery gave them a new adventure for play: "shell hunters."

In retrospect, the army offered a rationale for the buried ordnance. It reasoned that the hasty preparation of the grounds for a planned reconstruction of the plant probably resulted in much wreckage, including loaded shells, being pushed into the craters to facilitate the leveling of the surface.

8

A LONG LOOK FORWARD

A Fragile Peace, A New World War, A Cold War

The planning for the postwar world, which began prior to the armistice, was filled with hope that a just peace and well-laid plans for a new international order would diminish the prospects of another world conflict. However, the peace, if one would call it that, was ill conceived, poorly executed and placed in position or planted the seeds for the even greater worldwide clash that ensued a mere two decades later. Indeed, the redrawing of international boundaries with lines more to the designs of the drafters than suitable to the affected peoples created underlying factors for conflict that still plague the world today

Great Britain and France entered the peace talks principally focused on retribution rather than the recovery of their prostrated enemies. The mood and motivation of the two allies, along with a hint of their version of justice, can be extracted from the opening remarks of French president Raymond Poincare at the Paris Peace Conference:

> What it demands first, when it has been violated, are restitution and reparation for the peoples and individuals who have been despoiled or maltreated. It pursues a two-fold object—to render to each his due, and not to encourage crime through leaving it unpunished. What justice also

The World War I Middlesex Munitions Disaster

demands...is punishment of the guilty and effective guarantees against an active return of the spirit by which they were tempted.[1]

Not all of the Allied delegation agreed. John Maynard Keynes, one of the twentieth century's greatest economists, resigned from the British delegation in protest as he asserted that only a magnanimous peace that would not break Germany's future economic and financial viability would endure.

President Woodrow Wilson anticipated the end of the war as his opportunity to promote an environment that would preclude more great conflicts. Wilson's goals were outlined in his well-known "Fourteen Points." He spent the postwar months as a fervent advocate for his personal perspective of a just peace, a new world order and United States membership in the League of Nations. His tireless activity led to the breakdown of his health, which left him of questionable ability during the final two years of his presidency. The United States Senate's rejection of the league was the crushing blow to his heartfelt internationalist idealism. The United States, motivated by lessons from the Great War, would attempt to forestall its involvement in the next global conflict by the passage of a number of neutrality acts in the 1930s. The first, the Neutrality Act of 1935, barred shipments of war materials to belligerents and warned citizens that travel on ships of warring nations would be at their own risk. These generally ineffective provisions were terminated before the United States entered World War II.

Lessons learned from the Black Tom blast prompted the location of the region's major weapons shipping facility for World War II to then lightly settled areas of Monmouth County. When the Earle Naval Ammunition Depot was built in 1943–44, its inland storage area in Colts Neck was rural. Earle handled most of the weapons used at D-Day (June 6, 1944) and later operations in the European Theatre. Its magazines were built into hills or inside single-arch, earth-covered structures of reinforced concrete. Called igloos, they were designed to minimize the spread of an explosion. There was an extensive rail network inside the base that extended eastward to transport munitions to a pier in the Leonardo section of Middletown Township. While not as sparsely populated as Colts Neck, Leonardo was far from urban. The pier was built a considerable distance away from shore, a span that eventually reached 2.2 miles after expansions. The facility, later designated a naval weapons station, was named for Rear Admiral Ralph Earle, an ordnance specialist who was chief of the navy's Bureau of Ordnance during World War I.

The Earle base escaped World War II without a death from explosion.[2] Then, on April 30, 1946, a blast on the destroyer escort USS *Solar* at

135

Leonardo killed seven and injured scores. A naval inquiry into the origin claimed that the results were not conclusive, but the near-certain cause was the dropping on board of a "hedgehog," a small antisubmarine weapon that contained thirty-five pounds of Torpex, a volatile explosive. The death toll would have been higher if it were not for a commander's order made soon after the initial explosion to abandon the ship.[3]

The Black Tom disaster not only lingered in minds but also prompted renewed fears of enemy sabotage after this country entered the Second World War. President Franklin Delano Roosevelt is reported to have told John J. McCloy, his assistant secretary of war, when planning the internment of West Coast Japanese Americans, "We don't want any more Black Toms." The interned, however, were American citizens.

Disaster struck elsewhere during World War II. While this work is not a catalogue of the century's munitions explosions, one of the most tragic merits mention for its heavy toll, the reaction of survivors, the swift hand of punishment, charges of racism and the long campaign to set aside its investigation's findings. On July 17, 1944, an explosion at the Port Chicago Naval Magazine near Sacramento, California, killed 320 sailors and civilians while injuring nearly an additional 400. The majority of the casualties were enlisted African American sailors.

Well before the incident that became known as the Port Chicago disaster, issues were raised over the competency of the personnel, their leadership, training or lack of same, work regiments and the condition of equipment. Witnesses reported having heard at 10:18 p.m. a metallic sound and rending timbers, followed by a fire and explosion that destroyed the ship. The SS *E.A. Bryan* blew apart an adjoining vessel that was awaiting loading, the SS *Quinault Victory*, and shattered the pier, rail cars and equipment. Falling pieces of hot metal, ordnance and shattered glass caused numerous injuries and extensive damage along the base and in town. The deaths were limited to the pier area.

An extensive investigation was inconclusive but indicated that the likely cause was a munitions-handling error. After the accident, work conditions remained unchanged, which fanned widespread safety fears and led to work stoppages by 258 sailors. Their action became known as the Port Chicago mutiny. Attempts to secure their return to work divided the group, resulting in the convictions of 208 on a lesser charge of disobeying orders. The remaining 50 were court-martialed for mutiny, convicted and given long prison sentences. The convictions were affirmed following an appeal by future Supreme Court justice Thurgood Marshall, who was then special counsel for the NAACP Legal Defense Fund. Since after the war ended it was believed that their long-term confinement was no longer necessary to serve as an example of the consequences of disobeying orders, 47 of the 50 were released from prison in early 1946, while 2 remained in a navy hospital and 1 was confined for bad behavior. At the same time, the navy granted clemency to a large number of prisoners.

The case became a cause célèbre among African Americans as it highlighted racial inequality in the United States Navy and throughout the country's segregated armed forces. The Port Chicago mutiny was a stepping-stone to President Harry S Truman's integration of the military in 1948. The case dropped from the public eye but resurfaced in 1990 through an unsuccessful attempt in Congress to set aside the convictions. The Port Chicago Naval Magazine National Memorial was dedicated on the site in 1994. While a sailor who sought a pardon received one in 1994, most survivors believe that pardons free the guilty and they really deserved a more fitting form of exoneration. Efforts toward that end have not been successful.

Three decades later, memories of Morgan were still fresh in the minds of South Amboy residents, the passage of time and the intervention of a second world war notwithstanding. An active port had long filled the northeast section of the city, where in 1950 four piers and a barge tie-up rack extended into Raritan Bay. The easternmost pier, near the end of Augusta Street, handled oil. The largest, the coal-handling pier, was adjacent, while the narrow-bunker coal pier was located to the coal pier's west. South Amboy shipped a major supply of coal for metropolitan New York power and steam utilities. The other, Pier No. 4, which extended about 720 feet or fifteen freight car lengths into the bay, was essentially a railway trestle with a narrow walk along its side. After use over many years for the handling of explosives, this one was commonly called the "powder pier."

Knowledge about the dangers of explosives is gained from the investigation of accidents, which often result in the drafting of new safety standards. While they help, they are not always a remedy. In addition to the previously cited state and federal laws, South Amboy had its own munitions ordinance, while Interstate Commerce Commission rules regulated munitions transportation. However, the standards were not always followed.

The government of Pakistan had ordered a large shipment of anti-personnel and anti-tank mines from the Kilgore Manufacturing Company, while Morrison-Knudson Afghanistan, Inc., had ordered from Hercules Powder Company gelatin dynamite for shipment to that country. The dynamite, produced in Kenvil, New Jersey, and the mines from Newark,

Ohio, were to arrive at South Amboy for transfer by lighters to an oceangoing steamship, the Isbrandtsen Line's *Flying Clipper* at Gravesend Bay, New York, for the shipment to Pakistan. The commanding officer of the local Coast Guard district denied a permit for the loading or discharge of substantial amounts of explosives due to the nature of the hazard. The matter became urgent, as the material from Ohio was already en route, so special consideration was sought utilizing a revised plan to transfer the explosives to an anchorage near the navy's pier at Leonardo. The navy initially declined because the shipment was of a commercial nature. After an exemption was secured, the James Healing Corporation of Jersey City, an explosives-handling firm of over fifty years' standing that had extensive experience at South Amboy, was hired to transfer the mines and dynamite from the local powder pier. Healing sent four lighters to the site.

The transfer of the explosives began about 9:00 a.m. on Friday, May 19, 1950, about an hour after the dynamite and mines arrived by rail. By early evening, the equivalent of five and a half of seven railroad cars had been unloaded. At about 7:26 p.m., an explosion of tremendous force at the powder pier killed 31 Healing Company employees and 5 coal barge captains. In addition, over 350 residents of the Amboys were injured, many

An explosion during a cargo-handling job at the powder pier in South Amboy on May 19, 1950, was the second regional disaster with a heavy loss of life to occur in a generation. The event underscored the need to separate explosives from populated areas.

by broken glass. Remains from only a few bodies were recovered. The pier, the lighters and nearby railroad cars were destroyed, part of extensive property damage over a widespread area.[4]

The details of destruction and recovery are beyond the ambit of this work. However, it is probably needless to mention that local outcry was immediate and fervid. The Amboys were outraged over extensive destruction and grave personal risk from explosives twice in a generation.

After World War II, changing offensive weaponry brought new defenses for guarding our shores against attack. Coastal artillery mounted in fortified emplacements was supplanted by antiaircraft missiles as a response to long-range bombers having replaced naval vessels as the likely means of enemy incursions. Introduced in 1955, NIKE missile stations ringed numerous population centers, including New York. The New York City region command and control center was located in the hills above Sandy Hook in Middletown Township, a short distance from the Earle pier. Middlesex NIKE batteries were in place at Old Bridge and South Plainfield. NIKE stations, regularly installed in populated areas, were surrounded by a thirty- to forty-acre safety zone, one of the safety measures meant to assure residents that extensive safeguards precluded accidents.

Eight NIKE-AJAX missiles exploded on their launching pads at the Chapel Hill base, also in Middletown, on May 22, 1958, killing ten men. The accident, which occurred while new arming mechanisms were being installed, scattered pieces of warheads over a three-mile area. Although there had been NIKE accidents during tests, this was the first NIKE explosion at its launching pad. Described as the "accident that couldn't happen," the explosion heated up the Cold War in an area about a dozen miles from the former Gillespie plant.

IN THE REGION

The housing stock of Sayreville was influenced by the regional trend for ever-larger new houses after Oak Tree Village was built. The borough compares favorably with the nearby bayshore towns, where year-round occupancy of small seasonal homes in Laurence Harbor and Cliffwood Beach, a trend that began as the towns attempted to recover from the Great Depression, has resulted in strained communities. An unkind

The handsome former Sayre & Fisher Reading Room is a remaining testament of the firm's varied product and visual appeal of brick construction.

A remaining chimney is a memorial to the Sayre & Fisher firm that made the Sayreville community.

Mother Nature sent storms that wreaked havoc on their waterfronts and destroyed their recreational areas.

Sayreville retains a strong commercial base, although the borough has lost a significant part of its industry as part of a process experienced by the state of New Jersey and much of the Northeast. By 1987, the *Times* could headline a community profile (July 5), "Sayreville trades industry for bedroom-town image." After Hercules was sold, the plant closed. DuPont remains, but its activity and employment are much reduced. National Lead removed its plant but left its contamination. The enormous mixed-use residential-retail project named The Point is planned for reclaimed brownfields on the Raritan. If successful, The Point will elevate the town's retail profile and housing prices to unprecedented heights.

The importance of industry, the docks and the railroads diminished in South Amboy. After the city filled in its Raritan Bay waterfront, a "new and upscale neighborhood," according to the *Times* of June 30, 2002, was built and is virtually a town within the city. The higher-echelon place, Lighthouse Bay, has cultivated its own insularity, which has prompted rumblings for independence from the rough-and-ready old city to its west, but secession will not happen.

Morgan Beach has suffered the cruelest fate, as it is now closed from contamination from National Lead spoils that were deposited there. The issue of remediation was ongoing at publication.

Cheesequake Creek is lined with recreational boating facilities. It was home to the Luhrs Sea Skiff Company yacht-building works for decades. The reinforced road foundation for the Garden State Parkway has withstood the test of nearly sixty years.

Raritan Arsenal housed the Ordnance Specialist School from 1919 to 1941. Local officials agitated for its closure after the aforementioned explosion, but the base remained open until 1963. Following a massive cleanup, notably of World War II material, the area became the home of Middlesex Community College and Raritan Center, one of the largest business parks in the northeast. Its 13 million square feet embrace a variety of commercial uses and include the New Jersey Convention and Exposition Center.

The Raritan River Railroad enjoyed its peak passenger business during the World War I years, a time when its coaches were filled with munitions workers. This line, once the principal connection between South Amboy and New Brunswick, experienced a decline of patronage after the war, which led to its abandoning passenger service on April 16, 1938. It maintained a

A fragment of the powerhouse wall is one of few remaining structures from the Gillespie era. It is near the north bank of Cheesequake Creek on the premises of Brown's Boat Yard.

profitable freight operation as an independent short line until folded into Conrail in 1989.

The New Packer Hotel, which served as a place of refuge after the explosion, was later itself a tragic scene. On March 17, 1969, a fire that destroyed the building killed five and injured fourteen, according to the next day's *Times*.

Very little remains of the Gillespie plant. There is a commercial building in Morgan on the west side of Highway 35, a utility building in Brown's Boat Yard that was remodeled beyond recognition and, adjacent to it, a fragment of the powerhouse wall. Periodically, rumors surface that claim other structures survive, but the likelihood is small.

THE GILLESPIE LEGACY

While the Gillespie shell-loading plant was planned as one of the largest in the world, it had yet to attain its full production capacity, and its production spanned only several weeks. Short-term activity has not precluded extreme claims for the size of its output, often measured by its having produced a specified percentage of the shells used by the Allies on the western front. The percentage cited, deliberately omitted here, is grossly exaggerated. The British alone used a prodigious quantity of shells. In reality, the total Gillespie output would have supplied the British forces during one of the massive 1917 offensives for, perhaps, several days. The Gillespie Morgan production was even approached, according to Hunter, by Gillespie at Parlin, presumably California Loading Company, and Evans at Old Bridge, each of which loaded over 2 million shells.

Regarding loaded rounds, "by August, 1917, more artillery ammunition was on order with the French Government than was fired by the American Expeditionary Forces from January 18, 1918, when the first complete American division entered the line, until November 11, 1918."[5] In brief, the majority of shells fired by America were French made. The challenge of a new munitions industry's attempts to reach full productivity can be perceived by noting:

In artillery ammunition rounds of all calibers America at the end of the war was turning out unfilled shell faster than the French and nearly as fast as the British; but, due to the shortage in adapters and boosters, a shortage rapidly being overcome at the end of the war, the rate of production of completed rounds was only about one-third of either Great Britain or France.[6]

Looking at the big picture, while American industry can boast of the major accomplishment of rapidly building enormous and effective shell-loading plants, most of this nation's munitions contributions were raw materials. This fact does not diminish the American legacy because those materials, furnished in huge quantities, sustained the Allies' munitions industries. Indeed, having attained production levels in so short a span is a major testament to America's engineering and industrial capabilities. The American reach would have been even greater had the war continued into the next year, as one specification of a major Allied war council was "to bend energies toward a big American army in 1919 equipped with American supplies." In addition, American inventiveness was developing new offensive weapons that permitted Crowell to claim with confidence, "The expected American offensive in 1919 would have had its 'surprises' in numbers, some of which might well have proved to be decisive."[7] However, the Gillespie story is about sacrifice and forgetfulness.

The World War I Middlesex Munitions Disaster

As was noted, an effort to establish definitively how many died would almost certainly be futile. The initial reports were exaggerated, some to extremes. I thought at the start of my research that a death list might be constructed, but few names appeared in the press or other accounts. Many victims were not identified. Contemporary accounts not only indicated that some broken bodies could not be moved intact but also expressed the belief that others were destroyed into unrecognizable bits. Indeed, it is possible that some members of a transient labor force worked in anonymity or their families were unaware. I was presented with one story of a person who disappeared from family records around the time of the explosion; he was thought to have worked at Gillespie's and, according to a family in the dark, could have perished in the explosion. Casualties included rescue workers and bystanders, as well as plant workers. Even omitting possible increased mortality due to disease, I believe that at least one hundred died.

How could a tragic accident, one that took such a heavy human toll, slip from our collective memory? There is no short or simple explanation, but the research and writing of this book reinforced my belief that the event is hardly known at best but for practical purposes forgotten. Few residents in Sayreville, elsewhere in Middlesex County or in nearby Monmouth County who were questioned about the event had been aware of the Gillespie explosion. I have long been curious about both the event and memory lapse as a consequence of having lived the past forty years approximately twelve miles from the Gillespie site, while I grew up in Jersey City close to the better-remembered Black Tom explosion. Location, timing and cause contribute to the disparity in our collective memory. Black Tom was in plain sight of the New York media center. In addition, the loss by sabotage was an affront to both our professed neutrality and our national dignity. Black Tom may have become fixed in history because the investigation of this foreign intrigue was a historical detective adventure that was more gripping than fiction.

But with respect to Gillespie, most military accidents likely drift into forgetfulness. Wars, ostensibly about bravery and gallantry, make death in battle heroic. On the other hand, General George S. Patton reminded us that wars are won not by dying for one's country but by making the enemy die for his country. Accidents may be overlooked, as their dead are noncombatants, so their sacrifice drifts into the footnotes of war. Local pride should not take affront to history's having forgotten the Gillespie explosion since other domestic tragedies of World War I have similarly escaped memory. The forgetfulness process continued into the next Great War. In one especially egregious example, the cited July 17, 1944 Port Chicago, California ship-loading explosion was forgotten despite an even greater toll of 320 killed and 390 injured. The stain of racism and the miserable conditions under which a poorly trained workforce was compelled to labor turned a national tragedy into a national embarrassment.

Timing also contributed to the slippage of Morgan from memory. The disaster struck a mere five weeks before the armistice that concluded hostilities on November 11, its timing delayed while the shooting continued so the arrogant peacemakers could declare an end at the eleventh hour of the eleventh day of the eleventh month. The nation, eager for peace, was able to forget. After the isolationists rejected President Wilson's League of Nations, America appeared willing to let European affairs slip into our national subconscious. We were willing to permit the former European combatants to steer their course alone into the chasm that would erupt into a second world conflict little more than two decades later.

Just as the catastrophic event has been nearly forgotten, it is not surprising that memory of the sacrifice of the war's munitions workers has also faded. This largely unskilled and, for the most part, transient workforce labored in obscurity and at times died in anonymity. I was able to locate less than half of the explosion's deaths and had never seen an image of a casualty until this book was completed. The first was Andrew Kovalsky, pictured with his bride, Mary, the year before he died. Andrew was the son of Slovak immigrants, a skilled photographer who aspired to attain the next rung of success and dreamed of going West, at times while attired in his cowboy outfit. Almost certainly killed in the initial blast in 6-1-1, no identifiable

Andrew Kovalsky is pictured with his wife, Mary, at his wedding the year before he was killed in 6-1-1. Kovalsky, whose remains were never identified, provides a face to the Gillespie disaster. *Courtesy of Marie Labbancz.*

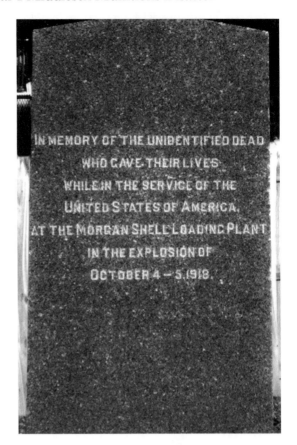

IN MEMORY OF THE UNIDENTIFIED DEAD
WHO GAVE THEIR LIVES
WHILE IN THE SERVICE OF THE
UNITED STATES OF AMERICA,
AT THE MORGAN SHELL LOADING PLANT
IN THE EXPLOSION OF
OCTOBER 4 – 5, 1918.

The monument to the victims stands in what is historically known as the Ernst Memorial Cemetery, located on the south side of Ernston Road a short distance west of Highway 9. *Courtesy of Joyce Elyea.*

body parts were ever found. His remains are interred in the mass grave of the unidentified. Two months later, his daughter was born. Henceforth, the disaster at Morgan will have a face along with its historical record.[8]

The mass grave of the unidentified, where a memorial was reportedly installed by the government shortly after the explosion, was unmarked by 1928. At that time, when the *South Amboy Citizen* campaigned for a proper monument, the dead were called heroes. The illustrated monument, erected at what is historically known as the Ernst Memorial Cemetery on Ernston Road, is believed to have been installed in 1929. The paper's editorial writer speculated on October 19, 1928, about what one of the Gillespie deceased might say if able to rise at a fitting memorial event on the forthcoming tenth anniversary of the armistice. After a word of thanks, the war worker might have observed, "We did not fight in France but we were killed in action, just as frightfully and just as bravely. But we have not died in vain."

NOTES

The accounts of the explosion and post-disaster relief efforts, drawn largely from contemporary news coverage, often omit footnotes to conserve space. The most thorough press coverage was given by the *New York Times* and the *Newark Evening News*.

Chapter 1

1. www.morgan-nj.org.
2. *Matawan Journal*, June 12, 1875; timetable to be effective July 1, 1875, Central Railroad of New Jersey, New York and Long Branch Division.

Chapter 2

1. Wall and Pickersgill, *History of Middlesex County.*
2. *Register*, November 7, 1894.
3. *National Cyclopedia of American Biography*, vol. 24.

CHAPTER 3

1. Munroe, *Regulation of Explosives.*
2. Wikipedia.org/wiki/sm_U53.
3. *Souvenir History Book,* quoted at bethlehemonline.com/bethsteel.html.
4. *New York Times,* various issues.
5. Munroe, *Regulations of Explosives.*
6. Ibid.

CHAPTER 4

1. Hunter, *History of Explosives.*
2. Committee on Military Affairs, *Miscellaneous Hearings.*
3. Venzon, *United States in the First World War.*
4. Crowell, *America's Munitions.*
5. Committee on Military Affairs, *Miscellaneous Hearings.*
6. Firestone, *Army Ordnance.*
7. Grier, *Shell Loading Plants.*
8. Hunter, *History of Explosives.*
9. *DuPont.*
10. Ibid.
11. Hunter, *History of Explosives.*
12. Williams, *Munitions Manufacture.*
13. Hammel, *Construction and Operation of a Shell Loading Plant,* accessed at amatol.atlantic.edu/amatol_book_home.html.
14. Hunter, *History of Explosives.*
15. *Matawan Journal,* December 27, 1917.
16. *War Expenditures,* in Google Books' *Collected Works of Sir Humphrey Davy.*
17. Firestone, *Army Ordnance.*
18. Ibid.
19. *New York Times,* August 27, 1917.
20. Department of Labor, *Report of the United States Housing Corporation.*
21. [New Brunswick] *Sunday Times,* October 6, 1918.

CHAPTER 5

1. *Perth Amboy Evening News*, October 6, 1918.
2. Larzelere, *Coast Guard in World War I*; and news accounts.
3. J.H. Duckworth, NEA staff correspondent, wrote the account of aviator Robert Shank likely published in various sources. See the *Asbury Park Evening News*, October, 10, 1918, under the headline "Like Flying Through Barrage…"
4. Assheton, *History of Explosions.*
5. [New Brunswick] *Daily Home News*, October 5, 1918.
6. Ibid.
7. *Newark Evening News*, October 5, 1918.
8. Yusko, *Morgan Explosion.*
9. Fleming, *Illusion of Victory.*

CHAPTER 6

1. *South Amboy Citizen*, December 7, 1918.
2. *Journal of the Engineers Club of Philadelphia* (February 1920).
3. Karcher, *New Jersey's Multiple Municipal Madness.*
4. Karcher, *Municipal History of the Borough of Sayreville.*

CHAPTER 7

1. Karcher, *Municipal History of the Borough of Sayreville.*

CHAPTER 8

1. Coetzee and Shevin-Coetzee, *World War I.*
2. Gabrielan, *Colts Neck.*
3. Gabrielan, *Middletown in the Twentieth Century.*
4. The National Board of Fire Underwriters and the Fire Insurance Rating Organization of New Jersey, *The South Amboy Port Explosion.*
5. Crowell, *America's Munitions.*

6. Ibid.
7. Ibid.
8. Author's conversation on September 6, 2012, with Marie Labbancz.

BIBLIOGRAPHY

Archives Search Report Findings for the Former T.A. Gillespie Loading Company, Morgan N.J. Rock Island, IL: United States Army Corps of Engineers, Rock Island District, 1994.

Assheton, Ralph. *History of Explosions on Which the American Tables of Distances Was Based: Including Other Explosions of Large Quantities of Explosives.* Wilmington, DE: Press of Charles H. Storey Company, 1930. [An extensive quote is in *Archives Search Report.*]

Coetzee, Frans, and Marilyn Shevin-Coetzee. *World War I: A History in Documents.* New York: Oxford University Press, 2002.

Committee on Military Affairs, U.S. Congress, Senate. *Miscellaneous Hearings, 1900–1919.* No. 3, *Investigation of the War Department*, part 3. 1918.

Crowell, Benedict. *America's Munitions, 1917–1918,* Washington, D.C.: Government Printing Office, 1919.

Department of Labor, United States. *Report of the United States Housing Corporation, War Emergency Construction.* Vol. 2. Washington, D.C.: Government Printing Office, 1919.

Duckworth, J.H. "Like Flying Through Barrage." *Asbury Park Evening News,* October, 10, 1918.

DuPont, The Autobiography of an American Enterprise. Wilmington, DE: E.I. DuPont de Nemours & Company, 1952.

Engineers' Club of Philadelphia. *Journal of the Engineers Club of Philadelphia* (February 1920).

Firestone, Clark B. *Army Ordnance, History of District Offices, New York.* Washington, D.C.: Government Printing Office, 1920.

Fleming, Thomas. *The Illusion of Victory, America in World War I.* New York: Basic Books, 2003.

Gabrielan, Randall. *Colts Neck.* Images of America. Charleston, SC: Arcadia Publishers, 1998.

———. *Middletown in the Twentieth Century.* American Century Series. Charleston, SC: Arcadia Publishers, 1999.

Grier, William D. "Shell Loading Plants, Proper Construction of Buildings and Handling of Materials." In *Live Articles on Special Hazards No. 8*, reprints from the *Weekly Underwriter, 1916–1917.* New York: Underwriter Printing and Publishing Co., 1917.

Hammel, Victor F. *Construction and Operation of a Shell Loading Plant and the Town of Amatol, New Jersey, for the United States Government Ordnance Department, U.S. Army.* New York: Atlantic Loading Company, 1919. Available online at amatol.atlantic.edu/amatol_book_home.html.

House of Representatives, 52nd Congress. *Report of the Board of Ordnance and Fortification.* Washington, D.C.: Government Printing Office, 1892.

Hunter, Major J. Herbert. *History of Explosives: Historical Record of Explosives in Relation to the Equipment of the United States Army.* Washington, D.C.: Government Printing Office, 1919.

The Journal of the Engineers' Club of Philadelphia and Affiliated Societies 37, no. 2 (February 1920).

Karcher, Alan J. *New Jersey's Multiple Municipal Madness.* New Brunswick, NJ: Rutgers University Press, 1998.

Karcher, Joseph T. *A Municipal History of the Borough of Sayreville New Jersey.* Boston, MA: Meador Publishing Co., 1958. [N.B. Karcher has been criticized for this and his companion *Township* work for a lack of citations. However, careful examination will reveal that his chronological notes are taken from official municipal records, perhaps supplemented by his personal recollections.]

———. *A Municipal History of the Township of Sayreville, 1876–1920.* Boston, MA: Meador Publishing Co., 1920.

Larzelere, Alex R. *The Coast Guard in World War I: An Untold Story.* Annapolis, MD: Naval Institute Press, 2006.

Munroe, Charles E. *Regulation of Explosives in the United States with Especial Reference to the Administration of the Explosives Act of October 6, 1917 by the Bureau of Mines,* Washington, D.C.: Government Printing Office, 1921.

National Board of Fire Underwriters and the Fire Insurance Rating Organization of New Jersey. *The South Amboy Port Explosion, South Amboy, N.J., May 19, 1950.* New York, n.d.

The National Cyclopedia of American Biography. Vol. 24. New York: James T. White & Co., 1935.

Riley, Thomas J. *Disaster Relief South Amboy, Perth Amboy and Nearby Communities in New Jersey Following Explosion in T.A. Gillespie Company Loading Plant at Morgan, New Jersey October 4–5, 1918.* New York, n.d. Typescript in collection of Sayreville Historical Society, reprinted serially in the *South Amboy Citizen*, October 10, 1968–March 6, 1969.

Sayreville Historical Society, Book Committee. *Sayreville.* Images of America, Charleston, SC: Arcadia Publishing, 2001.

Slesinski, Jason J. *A Cultural History of Sayreville.* Sayreville, NJ: Ultra Media Publications, 2011.

Snyder, John P. *The Story of New Jersey's Civil Boundaries, 1606–1968.* Trenton, NJ: Bureau of Geology and Topography, 1969.

Souvenir History Book of the Borough of South Bethlehem, Pennsylvania. South Bethlehem, PA, 1915. Quoted online at bethlehemonline.com/bethsteel.html.

Venzon, Anne Cipriano. *The United States in the First World War: An Encyclopedia.* New York: Garland Publishers, 1995.

Wall, John P., and Harold E. Pickersgill. *History of Middlesex County, 1664–1920.* New York: Lewis Historical Publishing Company, 1921.

War Expenditures, Hearings before Subcommittee No. 5 (Ordnance) Select Committee on Expenditures in the War Department, House of Representatives, Sixty-Sixth Congress. Washington, D.C.: Government Printing Office, 1919. Available in Google Books' *Collected Works of Sir Humphrey Davy.*

Williams, William Bradford. *Munitions Manufacture in the Philadelphia Ordnance District.* Philadelphia, PA: Williams, 1921.

Yusko, Frank. *The Morgan Explosion of 1918: The Documentary Film.* Milltown, NJ: Visionary Video Studios, 2009.

WEBSITES

Many websites were consulted for casual reference. One merits an extended look for detailed, insightful information about Morgan: www.morgan-nj.org, known as "All About Morgan."

INDEX

ABOUT THE AUTHOR

Randall Gabrielan is the executive director of the Monmouth County Historical Commission and that county's historian. He has written many books of history on five counties in two states. This is his second Middlesex title. He has also spoken widely on a variety of topics. Gabrielan lives about twelve miles from the explosion site with his wife, Carol T. Stout, and their golden retriever, Roland.